THE LOSS
OF
COMMON SENSE
IN
MODERN
AMERICAN
CULTURE

TOM S. PANE

THE LOSS OF COMMON SENSE IN MODERN AMERICAN
CULTURE

ISBN: 979-8-33023-440-0

Table Of Contents

Preface — i

Chapter 1 — Early American Idealism, Government Growth — 1

Chapter 2 — Easter Surprise! Who Is This Author? — 15

Chapter 3 — Changing Paths: Dashing Through Life — 25

Chapter 4 — Behavioral Addictions: Our Best Friends — 37

Chapter 5 — Religion And Politics: Do They Fit Together? — 51

Chapter 6 — Capitalism, Politicians, And Corporations — 67

Chapter 7 — Education For Life: Then And Now — 95

Chapter 8 — Happiness And The Magic Mirror — 101

Chapter 9 — Introspection Or Us Versus Them — 109

Chapter 10 — Recent Past Presidents — 129

Chapter 11 — Summary And Analysis: Is This The End? — 147

Epilogue — 201

Bibliography — 203

Notes — 205

Preface

This is not a book that many American citizens, politicians, or corporations might like. It is not politically correct and what is written might be opposed by both far-right conservative Republicans and far-left liberal Democrats. With the way today's political and social opinions have become so extreme, this book may be hated to such an extent that people might be willing to seek me out, threaten me, or do me harm. We are living in extreme tribal times where some people believe that anyone who is not like them is an evil or bad person. I do not want to be another victim of negative social threats, so I am using a pseudonym.

Some of this book was written before the COVID-19 pandemic. The way this virus spread and the severe consequences and deaths it created occurred because many people have disregarded the long-term significance of maintaining a healthy body and the compromising dialog that is necessary for social stability.

When I first started writing this book, I looked around the world and wondered: "Why are there countries on Earth where the general populations are both healthier and happier? Does it occur because their leaders provide the citizens with health and economic benefits not found in the United States? Or is it that many of our citizens no longer believe or want to follow the Era of Enlightenment philosophies and social norms that guided Our Founding Fathers when they created the country?"

When people choose hyperbolic, technological-based philosophies and ideals as their new normality, many Americans become so mesmerized and demanding to satisfy their wanting behaviors that they seem to lose sight of what these new ideologies may be doing to their overall mental outlook. Common sense and rationale become lost practices when believing, desiring, and acting out what the addictive media and Internet prescribes become a new biblical norm for defining the culture. Life becomes a rocket ship ride of data, colors, and unlimited choices where everyone is trying to outdo everyone else. But where are these self-induced overdoses of technology, data, and extremism taking us?

Chapter 1

EARLY AMERICAN IDEALISM, GOVERNMENT GROWTH

In January of 1776, Thomas Paine published a pamphlet called "Common Sense." Paine was one of the most-read writers of the 18th century. Decades before numerous human rights laws were enacted in our country, Paine advocated and supported antislavery, animal rights, women's rights, and free public education. A major aspect of this "Common Sense" pamphlet talked about why the common people in the American colonies should challenge and seek independence from the English Monarchy. Paine focused on why the separation from England should occur, and his pamphlet was one of the major factors influencing the colonists to fight in the American Revolution.

Merriam-Webster Dictionary defines common sense as "sound and prudent judgment based on a simple perception of the situation or facts." Some words that are synonyms of common sense are discreetness, discretion, level-headedness, prudence, sensibleness, and wisdom. Common sense, judgment, and wisdom mean the ability to reach intelligent conclusions. Sense implies a reliable ability to judge and decide with soundness, prudence, and intelligence. Common sense suggests an average degree of such ability without sophistication or special knowledge. Common sense tells me it is wrong or right. Judgment implies a sense of temperament, refined by experience, training, and maturity. These are all Merriam-Webster denoted interpretations.[1]

Many of the above ways of defining common sense do not seem common or sensible in both today's social and governmental functioning abilities. The origin of the words "common sense" may have started in the aftermath of England's Glorious Revolution. The concept then moved to the French Era of Enlightenment and finally to the Age of Revolution in the American colonies with Thomas Paine.

In the 14th Century, common sense was originally the power of uniting the impressions conveyed by the five physical senses, thus, ordinary understanding, without being foolish or insane. (Latin "*sensus communis*," Greek "*aisthesis*," meaning "good sense," is from 1726.)[2]

To me, in present day psychology, there are two types of common sense.

1) Historical Common Sense. In determining one's choices, the perceptions and analyses of one's options by using reason, wisdom, and rationale to figure out what is most appropriate for a given situation. This method has hardly changed throughout many generations of history going back to the Ancient Greeks or further.

2) Common Sense based on the current social variability of the times. Perceptions and choices are based on and influenced by the latest social activities, fads, peer pressures, and trends in music, movies, television, advertising, fashion, etc., that do not use reason or rationale to be accepted or understood within one's life experiences. I call these the "here today, gone tomorrow" approaches toward today's common-sense perception and usage.

The strangest thing about historical Common Sense is that in much of today's American culture, historical Common Sense is hardly common. If you were to say that a sense of extremism is common, or a sense of tribalism is common, or a sense of greed is common, I would say you are closer to describing American culture today.

A major aspect of historical Common Sense in America was defined by how people lived and developed their daily habits, and their value systems based on positive religious morals and ethics. You can be both religious and spiritual without belonging to a specific organized religion.

Let us look at one of the greatest and most durable generations in American history. These were the generations born between 1890 and 1930. This was the generation of both my parents and grandparents. In many ways, life was a struggle for many people who were born during this time frame. A lot of people came from farms to the big cities, or they came to America from other countries. They then had to learn how to adapt to big city life and the cultures of a new country.

Decisions leading up to Prohibition, World War I, the Roaring 20's, and the start of the Great Depression were developed, decided, and administered by people born before 1880. President William Taft was born in 1857, President Woodrow Wilson was born in 1856, President Warren Harding in 1865, President Calvin Coolidge in 1872, and President Herbert Hoover in 1874. These gentlemen were Presidents of the United States between 1908 and 1933.

As an example, General John Pershing, who was Commander of the American Expeditionary Force on the Western Front of Europe during World War I, was born in 1860. These men were not the greatest innovative or rational leaders this country has seen. There were many formative and challenging events that took place while they were President or leading our military. Most of these leaders either did not do enough to solve our country's problems or did too much, which created more problems.

It was not until the early 1930s, when Franklin Roosevelt became President in the early days of the Depression and led us through most of World War II, that the strengths of those in the Greatest Generation blossomed. This Generation saw the necessity to pick themselves up after the sorrows and losses of the Depression and a worldwide war with tens of millions of soldiers and civilians killed. They were named the Greatest Generation because of how their leadership decisions were based on using positive ethical and moral foundations to guide the country.

Back in the 1930s, great numbers of people fell into poverty, which was displayed to the world by their skinny bodies and worn faces that often looked ten to twenty years older than their actual age. Medicaid and

Medicare were not available, and Social Security had just started giving people insufficiently small amounts of money to live on. Fast forward to the 2005-9 financial recession or the Covid-19 pandemic. A poor person could now have healthcare coverage, receive welfare checks and food stamps, own smart phones, computers, flat-screen TVs, and maybe even a vehicle to drive. Large numbers are overweight or obese. America may have some of the fattest people living in poverty in the world.

What happens to deciphering the rationality of Common Sense when it goes from one's outlook being based on positive morals and ethics, the historical norms, to one's outlook based on "what is awesome and trendy?"

Just because events around you are "common" does not make them an aspect of Common Sense. Here is a more current example of what I mean. Your current cell phone is a couple of years old but still works fine. Maybe you do not want to feel left out, so you go out and buy one of those newer, expensive smartphones, though this purchase might not be what is currently best for your family budget. But all your friends have one of these phones, and you do not want to feel left out for not having the latest technology. You put the charged amount on your 15-30% credit card and bring it home. You may have thought this was an overall, common-sense approach until you got home. Your purchase may upset your wife, who now either wants one of these newer smartphones for herself or realizes your purchase is way outside the family budget, and with the added interest you would be paying a lot more for the device. Your children may be irate that they are not allowed to have a phone like yours to communicate with all their friends. Maybe you realize that what others call Common Sense approaches with their purchases may not be the right kind of Common Sense for you and the family.

How about we expand this example to a bigger question? Maybe there is a leader in power whose governmental decisions produce lower unemployment rates; it may get you a small raise in income or make your stock investments increase in value. This leader speaks of how powerful the country has become under his leadership, and he promises to keep the country the strongest in the world, both economically and militarily.

Maybe you question some of the leader's tactics, biases, and negative language toward minorities, people of other races, or those in different political parties because of your own religious beliefs or the family ethics of how you were raised by your parents.

But do you use your new Internet-inspired Common Sense to rationalize that by supporting this leader, you might soon be able to buy more stuff for yourself, spend more on the kids, take your wife out to fancier restaurants, or get new electronic gadgets for everyone in the household? Was the ability to acquire more "stuff" a primary reason why our Founding Fathers chose to create and develop our new country? The true and historical meaning of Common Sense used by our Founding Fathers was advocated to create more equality and harmony in how people related to each other. Buying more stuff does not produce greater equality for everyone.

In the 1920s and 1930s, both Hitler and Mussolini initially presented their people with promises of superior military power, greater and richer employment opportunities, putting more food on their dinner tables, the ability to buy more stuff for themselves, better public services, and transportation facilities. The people in each country used their "go along with the crowd common sense" to dismiss their leader's discriminatory tactics against minorities, their preaching against those other "evil" political parties, and their downgrading and imprisonment of other ethnic races.

In Italy, eventually, Fascism became not only acceptable to the public but a desired way for the leader to govern. In Germany, the people eventually favored the Nazi propaganda approach of a totalitarian state. In both countries, the people's common-sense approaches falsely rationalized that antisemitism and anti-parliamentarism were acceptable behaviors. The form and usage of their common-sense approach allowed them to believe that the white Aryan race and nationalism were necessary for military strength and greater financial security, thereby giving them the opportunity to do and buy more. Hitler created "Fuhrerprinzip," the "leader principle," where subordinates were committed to absolute obedience to the leader. Hitler also held that both the party structure and the branches of the government were subservient to the leader at the top.[3]

There are some politicians in America who run for office who believe that, if elected, they would have the authority to replace any current short-or-long-term governmental worker who does not fully believe in the ideologies of that ruler and replace them with people who only believe in the ideologies of the candidate who won the election. This political desire comes from the same "so-called common-sense approach" followed by the citizens of Germany and Italy in the 1930s.

History shows us that this pattern of manipulating mass populations repeats itself around the globe every so many decades. Because generations die and newer generations become more removed from negative past experiences, they lose interest in their city, state, or country's history and what they could learn from comparing the historical past to the present.

Fascism and Nationalism are not governmental ruling philosophies that just suddenly occur within any nation. They usually start out as "lite" versions that involve subjecting the populace to a lot of subtle brainwashing propaganda from a leader or organization over time. They could start with police or troops arresting protesters who may be demonstrating against government inaction or injustices. A leader might call the protestors terrorists, and then repeat the claim that they are trying to destroy the government that only he is trying to keep together. He will insist that physical force might have to be used against foreigners to save and stabilize the government. It is only his methods of law and order that must prevail. He instills fear in the public that these foreigners and evil radicals must be removed or locked up so that good citizens will be safe and not have their homes and businesses robbed or burned to the ground.

Then there is the propaganda that these so-called troublemakers want to create a socialist government that would destroy the great economy that he will create or that he has already created. Shifting the blame on why these current "evil" situations are occurring is a prime tool for a leader to use to convince the citizens that the only solution to all their problems is that he should be the country's leader. Of course, many of the problems may have occurred under his leadership, but he disregards that responsibility, blaming it on local radicals, leftist propaganda, or foreign intervention. If you want to learn more about how Fascism and Nationalism developed in Europe and around the world during the 1920s and 1930s, watch the British Documentary called "Impossible Peace – the Time Between World Wars" on Acorn TV or Acorn streaming through Amazon.

FOUNDING FATHERS GOVERNMENT

Our Founding Fathers set up our government differently than other countries in the world. The Founders had no idea what the daily lifestyle activities or customs of future generations might be. Their efforts were in constructing a form of government that might treat the citizens differently than the old monarchs, dictators, or aristocratic governments seen around the world. From the very beginning, our leaders would sit down together, whatever their backgrounds were, and discuss, in an open exchange of ideas, the suggestions that the various colonial representatives brought to the meetings from the citizens in their districts. There were no political parties, just educated patriots who saw the importance of starting a new country, a country that could be developed for the benefit of everyone.

There were not hundreds or thousands of lobbyists influencing our leaders with large campaign contributions for their constant reelection. These early representatives intended to serve our country in governmental leadership jobs for short periods of time, not to become permanent or long-serving political dynasties. Most of our Founding Fathers' philosophical governing ideas, which they incorporated into the Declaration of Independence, the Constitution of the United States, and the Bill of Rights, came from both the philosophies of the Eras of French Enlightenment and the Scottish Enlightenment that were taking hold in Europe.

The Age of Enlightenment was a late 17th and early 18th-century intellectual movement emphasizing reason, individualism, and skepticism. It also incorporated the then-modern idea of progress through reason and science. The Enlightenment philosophies became the basis of the American Revolution. From these French and English philosophers came the following ideas:

John Locke

>-Governmental power from the consent of the people

>- Creating a representative government

>- Establishing the limits of governmental powers

Charles Montesquieu

>-The importance of separation of powers

>-The Federal system of governing

>-The three branches of government

>-The system of checks and balances

Jean Jacques Rousseau

>-Direct democracy

Voltaire

>- Free Speech, religious tolerance

American thinkers of the 1700s, including Thomas Paine, James Madison, Thomas Jefferson, John Adams, and Benjamin Franklin, heavily emphasized Scottish philosophical thinking in helping to create a new form of governing. They accepted not only the anti-authoritarian doctrine of liberalism, but also spoke of the importance of being virtuous, enlightened, and community-focused, which they called Republican Thinking. There was a lot of skepticism about the American Enlightenment, with people remembering Plato's belief that democracy led to tyranny, and Aristotle's belief that democracy was the best of the worst forms of government. Who were the teachers of some of Our Original Founders? At 16 years old, Thomas Jefferson attended William and Mary College, where he was mentored by William Small, a highly respected member of the Scottish Enlightenment and a leading educator at the school.

James Madison, who attended Princeton in 1769, was mentored by John Witherspoon, who was part of a group of educators from Scotland that brought the ideas of the Scottish Enlightenment to the Colonies.

Alexander Hamilton attended Kings College, today's Columbia, where he was tutored by Robert Harpur, who came from Glasgow, Scotland. Many of Our Founders were well-versed and educated in understanding Aristotle, Cicero, and the Bible, often reading these manuscripts in their original languages. To show you the significance of the Scot John Witherspoon, he mentored 28 U.S. Senators, 49 U.S. Representatives, 3 Supreme Court Justices, and 12 governors while teaching in our country.

Benjamin Franklin, going back to his day of the Poor Richard's Almanac, held that to live a "useful and dignified" life, a person should exhibit the virtues of temperance, silence, order, resolution, frugality, industry, sincerity, justice, moderation, cleanliness, tranquility, and humility. These were the principles he believed made a good citizen. Today, Americans are reminded that temperance, frugality, moderation, tranquility, and humility might be anti-capitalistic and bad for the economy. Today we might be told to be enthusiastic, constantly excited, big spenders, debtors, braggers, and social climbers to be successful and "get ahead."

Do most of today's Americans know what philosophies and beliefs some of Our Founding Fathers valued? How about the words in the publication Federalist #10, used by James Madison on November 23, 1787?

"A zeal for different opinions concerning religion, concerning government, and many other points, as well of speculation as a practice; an attachment to different leaders ambitiously contending for preeminence and power; or to persons of other description whose fortunes have been interesting to the human passions, have, in turn, divided mankind into parties, inflaming them with mutual animosity, and rendered them much more disposed to vex and oppress each other than to cooperate for their common good....But the most common and durable source of factions has been the various and unequal distribution of property. Those who hold and those who are without property have ever formed distinct interests in society. Those who are creditors, and those who are debtors, fall under a like discrimination...It is in vain to say that enlightened statesmen will be able to adjust these clashing interests and render them all subservient to the public good. Enlightened statesmen will not always be at the helm."[4] In this publication, Madison also said: "No man is allowed to be a judge in his own cause because his interest would certainly bias his judgment." After serving two terms as President, George Washington said this during his Farewell Address in 1796: "One of the expedients of (a) party to acquire influence within particular districts is to misrepresent the opinions and aims of other districts. You cannot shield yourselves too much against the jealousies and heart burnings which spring from these misrepresentations. They tend to render alien to each other those who ought to be bound together by fraternal affection. Let me now take a more comprehensive view and warn you in the most solemn manner against the baneful effects of the spirit of (a) party generally. The alternate domination of one faction over another, sharpened by the spirit of revenge natural to party dissension, which in different ages and countries has perpetrated the most horrid enormities, is itself a frightful despotism. But this leads at length to a more formal and permanent despotism.

The disorders and miseries which result gradually incline the minds of men to seek security and repose in the absolute power of an individual, and sooner or later the chief of some prevailing faction, more able or more fortunate than his competitors, turns this disposition to the purpose of his own elevation on the ruins of public liberty…Harmony, liberal intercourse with all nations are recommended by policy, humanity, and interest. But even our commercial policy should hold an equal and impartial hand, neither seeking nor granting exclusive favors of preferences. There can be no greater error than to expend or calculate upon real favors from nation to nation."

Washington's words about political parties have become very prophetic in modern American culture. Maybe before running for political office, politicians should be required to verify that they will first represent what is best for the average citizen and, secondly, what is best for corporations. When they take their oath of office, maybe it should include a promise by them to be moral, ethical, and fair in how they will compromise with each other for the good of the populace.

Read any of the writings of numerous Founding Fathers. You might notice that religious and moral integrity were viewed as extremely important in how they wanted the new country's politicians and administrators to act and function while doing their civic duties for the country.

Look around America today. Do you see our current politicians using similar morals and ethics when they talk about members of the opposing parties?

STRENGTHS OF AMERICAN PIONEERS 1800

Do you think most of the people in today's American society have the mental fortitude or physical stamina that our early pioneers had after the American Revolution? Though our average lifespans today might be longer because of medical advances and drugs, we seem to have lost a lot of the moral sense of how to treat each other with respect. We also do not seem very dedicated to seeing that our youth get a balanced education based on positive moral and ethical responsibilities. We have become a divergent society more concerned about "ME rather than WE."

Our ancestors succeeded with a positive, forgiving, and intellectual perspective based on the fundamentals of ancient religious beliefs. Many of the beliefs and goals in modern American lifestyles seem to be almost the opposite of what was believed and daily practiced by our early Founders and pioneering explorers. The modes of common decency, comprehensive studying and learning, productive physical work, an appreciation of nature, and a proper utilization of our natural environment played significant roles in early American life.

Early American pioneers valued teaching children at a young age by instilling in them the wisdom and maturity that would come from educating themselves through books, interpersonal physical contact with skilled workers and educators, and spending time practicing those skills on their own. There were no quick fixes or "Dummies Guides" to learning and developing those skills. The respect for one's parents and grandparents became a fundamental and natural principle for early America's pioneering children.

Prior to the U.S. Constitution, in 1787, Article 3 of the Northwest Ordinance, the Congress of the Confederation stated: "Religion, morality, and knowledge, being necessary to good government and the happiness of mankind, schools, and the means of education shall forever be encouraged."[5] This is also stated in Article 8 of the Michigan Constitution.

If you read many of the writings of our Founding Fathers, these three aspects of life, along with ethics, civic-mindedness, thrift, self-control, and patience, were what being free in this new country meant. Practicing these positive virtues in your daily life created a philosophical and emotional roadmap to being an appreciative citizen of this new country.

After the passage of the Northwest Ordinance, a group of New Englanders got together and prepared to establish a new settlement in what is now Ohio. At the time, this area constituted the "northwest" part of the United States. The Ohio area was a raw, wild country with numerous Indian tribes living there. It took about three months of difficult travel by horse, wagon, and barge to get from Massachusetts to the area that was going to be a new settlement on the northern banks of the Ohio River. They called the area Marietta. People of various skills: farmers, businessmen, craftsmen, and their families slowly kept arriving. The forests needed to be chopped down to create a town, and properties needed to be cleared for homes and farms. Imagine cutting down 5-to 6-foot-wide trees with axes and manual saws, cutting planks, framing and building homes, and fencing their properties. This work was done by men and teens of all ages.

The women worked as hard as men, dealing with their own responsibilities. In his book "The Pioneers," David McCullough describes the life early pioneering women faced and the tasks they accomplished. The center of pioneer life was the home where a woman's work was never done. There were no days off, no vacations.

"Besides cooking, baking, cleaning, and the full-time role of wife and mother, there were cows to milk, gardens to tend, candles and soap to be made, butter to churn…Butter was a major element of the frontier diet, and making good butter was a skill in which women took special pride.

Then there was yarn to spin, wool to weave, clothes to make for large families, clothes to wash, mend and patch. And just as the man of the house had his ax, plowshare, long rifle, and other tools necessary for the work to be faced, so, too, did the woman of the house: knives, needles, spoons, paddles, hickory brooms, spinning wheels, and most important, the bulbous heavy iron pots to be seen in nearly every cabin."[6]

I do not think that there is any way to compare the duties and tasks of early American women to today's city/suburban housewives and mothers. Today, most women have cars, washers and dryers, grocery stores, telephones, and computers, to ease many tasks. When modern-day families have a good income, they may have someone periodically clean their homes or use self-propelled gadgets to do some of the cleaning. Why cook when you can buy something premade, pop it into the microwave or oven, or just buy "fast food" takeouts like burgers, fried chicken, or pizzas on your way home from work? If you have the money, you can pay someone to care for your preschool and school-aged children while you are at work.

Making your own clothes, you got to be kidding. There's Amazon or other companies where you can order anything you might want, and it will be delivered right to your front door.

But what about the women in America who do not have all those economic privileges? What about the millions of women who are not like the image of those so-called average city/suburban women you see on most daytime and nighttime soap opera television programs? How about the women living on small rural farms or far into the woods or mountains? Rural life in America is nothing like what you might see on Hallmark Channel's "When Calls the Heart" TV show where every citizen has perfectly polished, white-toothed smiles, where every woman wears a different, perfectly matching outfit every day of the year and every family problem is solved in a day or two.

Poor rural women with families and other women with laborious, low-paying jobs are like the early pioneer women of the 1800s. The hardships they often endure barely get recognized and appreciated by city folks.

Then there is the subject of women not being allowed to vote because men did not see them as equals. The women's suffrage amendment to the United States Constitution was first proposed in Congress starting in 1878 but was not passed until 1919. It took 41 years to convince legislative men that women were just as capable of deciding who should serve as their President and representatives in government. But women were denied the right to vote for 128 years since the U.S. Constitution was established.

The lifestyles of many of the people who live and work in rural America are barely seen in modern American television shows. CBS was a big factor in what was called the "Rural Purge" of American television. Though many of the hillbilly and cowboy shows were very popular in the

1950s-60s, TV executives dropped those programs and favored showing city/suburbia lifestyles that were more young, hip, and urban.

As a result, in the 1970s, single parent families and divorces became common themes in television programs. Production companies also realized that "Sex Sells" and it opened the gates to pushing the boundaries of acceptable behaviors until there were almost no limitations on what could be shown, especially if someone was willing to pay extra to watch it.

Many parents do not understand, nor do they seem to care, what types of videos their children are able to watch on the internet. Smartphone communications among our youth have taken the place of in person, relationship building experiences between males and females. Sharing heart felt emotional experiences that lead to lasting romantic relationships take time and devotion. Texting isn't a substitute for deep interpersonal exchanges.

Young women seem to understand this better than young men. Maybe this is one of the factors why the number of women in college exceeds the number of men. Many are finding that having a career will enhance their opportunities to find partners or husbands for lasting relationships based on mutual respect, stability, and companionship.

Male social development might be enhanced by eliminating sexual videos as personal entertainment experiences. These videos are often used as substitutes for developing strong personal relationships with women. Using sexual fantasies can corrupt the most important foundations of successful, lasting relationships.

The internet has also become a mechanism where many women are being swindled out of large amounts of money by corrupt men acting as potential loving companions. Today, both men and women are being deceived because people may be looking for love in all the wrong places. Relying on fantasies to achieve fulfillment is one of the first steps on one's way to eventual divorce.

The following chapter starts with a fictional story which might be seen as a future Twilight Zone show. The chapter will also explain some of the early common-sense events in my life that recently encouraged me to write this book.

Chapter 2

EASTER SURPRISE! WHO IS THIS AUTHOR?

It is a couple of years into the future. The latest national elections had turned into a frenzy of irrational political tribalism never seen in American history. Voters not only disagreed with anyone of the opposing party but often viewed them as Satanic, cultish, or socialistic communists. For a month before Easter, a strange pink cloud hovered miles above the United States Capitol Building in Washington, D.C., perplexing all three branches of government and the United States Military. People were questioning whether it was a UFO or some type of strange Russian spy device.

On Easter Sunday morning the cloud started descending towards the Capitol until it came to rest on the National Mall grass. Music that sounded like warbling harps could now be heard coming from the pink cloud. With hundreds of news cameras recording every second of the event, a man who looked like a hippy from the 1960s emerged from the cloud dressed in clothing from 2000 years ago, and he started to speak. "I am a messenger, and I come in peace, but with a heavy heart. Why are you so angry with each other? Your inner anger foments the spreading of more senseless violence among yourselves.

Do you not realize that your overconsumption of natural resources is destroying the planet? Why are you not considering the environmental quality you are leaving for future generations? Why are you teaching your children that striving for the unlimited accumulation of wealth and materialism is more important than anything else? Why not share this planet's wealth more equally among all its inhabitants for greater worldwide harmony? Think more holistically about your children's health and well-being. Be kind and love everyone because they are all your neighbors. For life's bountifulness, credit yourselves and your family instead of your cards."

The messenger stepped back into the cloud, and soon, the cloud started its journey back into the sky. The cloud rose higher and higher until it looked like a small dot in the sky when suddenly a rocket was seen speeding toward the cloud. The explosive impact created a brilliant flash of red light against the blue sky's background.

Suddenly, on all TV screens across the United States, the President appeared and announced, "A socialist or communist organization has created a sleight of hand illusionary propaganda trick to try and destroy American capitalism and our economic lifestyle. The United States functions best when all our citizens want and have more of everything as their primary goals in life. We cannot allow outsiders to propose for us to accept Socialist ideals. Your government must take strong actions against any entity which advocates favoring humanity over prosperity."

As the crowds walked away from The Mall, they opened their wallets to make sure that their charge cards were still there, and they smiled when they saw them, knowing they could continue to think about what to buy next. No person or entity was going to stop their behavioral practices of wanting it all.   (To be continued later in the book.)

Most Americans are going to hate this book. For some, reading it might remind you of a moral or ethical lecture rightfully given to you in the past by your mother, grandmother, or maybe even a great-grandmother concerning their observation of your questionable behaviors toward yourself or others. Or this book may remind you of a very emotional and reflective experience you might have had when you were looking at yourself in a mirror. Maybe instead of seeing your makeup, hairstyle, or style of clothing, one day you saw a reflection of your soul, or your innate moral compass, and you did not like what you saw.

Maybe these "other" images created new introspections about what you were doing with your life or how you were treating yourself, your friends, or your family. Maybe you started asking yourself, "Why am I acting this way?" or "Why am I creating this false façade that others may think is the real me?" Morality and ethics are not things that you can go out and buy when you have the desire. You earn them when you practice using them every day.

What you will be reading in this chapter describes some of the basic activities, responsibilities, and cooperative efforts within families that existed in America since the early days of the republic. Obviously, life has become more complex and materialistic, but family relationships remain relatively like earlier times. After many extensive discussions with both my parents, grandparents, and relatives about their family lives as far back as they can remember, certain elements have stood out as primary foundational factors that support a strong, coherent family. But there are also factors that do the opposite, creating disharmony which can cripple and even destroy some family relationships.

I was born in 1949. My parents could not afford to buy their own house, so we lived with my mother's parents on the first floor of their two-flat apartment building in one of the biggest cities in America. My grandparents were born in the 1880s in Eastern Europe, Grandma lived on a farm and Grandpa lived in a nearby small town. Though there was a city public school about two blocks from where I grew up, our family was Catholic, so I attended the Catholic parochial school, kindergarten through eighth grade.

The nuns from the parish convent were great. They were not concerned about debating the school district for new teacher contracts every couple of years. It seemed their primary focus was devoted to educating the students as well as they could. For most of the eight years of grammar school, we walked eight or so blocks to school. The school did not have a lunch program, so you either brought a simple sandwich in a paper bag and maybe a piece of fruit, or you quickly walked home for a quick lunch and then went back to school for the afternoon classes. My parents happened to keep the yearly class group pictures from my seventh and eighth grades. I recently found those two pictures, and you had to hunt to find any overweight children in my classes. There were only a few.

Throughout grade school, after school ended for the day, we boys met up at that public school's recreation area that surrounded the public-school building to play games and baseball by ourselves. There were no parents around except in the seventh and eighth grades, where there was one local Little League baseball team, but most boys, since there were so many of us, played in a minor league conference. We did not have uniforms; we only had a same-colored baseball cap with two letters signifying our conference. Different teams had different colored caps. A parent would be a coach; either one of the coaches or a visiting parent would be the umpire. Games would be on a Saturday or on a weekday after dinner when there was still a lot of daylight available. The baseball field would just be a field of grass at a city park, and someone would pace off the bases and stick them into the grass. There were no outfield fences or bleachers, and few parents attended the games.

But for most afternoons on weekdays after school and on Saturdays, we kids would just gather at that local public school to play. We would choose team captains, and the captains would alternately pick their team players. We would use chalk to mark the ground where the bases and home plate would be. The playing field was a hard surface, tiny stones over a hardpacked tarred surface. Skinned knees and elbows were a common result when we slipped or fell while running the bases. We brought our own mitts, balls, and bats if we had them. If someone didn't have their own equipment, we shared equipment with the other boys. We did not keep track or have a record of which team won or lost, and the captains and team players changed every day. There were never any trophies for winners or depressed feelings for losers. We played because it was fun.

For basketball, we would gather at a friend's house that had a hoop attached to the family garage. There were only a few homes that had attached hoops. For football, we played at a neighbor's property, which included an extra grassy lot. Later, we played at a small public park.

Equipment was the barest minimum, like one deteriorating football and a cheap helmet. Each team had three to five players. The kids themselves did the organizing and rulemaking and made up their own plays. (Side note: When I played organized football against other schools during my freshman year in high school, our issued team helmets were all old secondhand leather helmets.)

When we were not playing a sport, we were bicycling all over the neighborhood, each year extending our biking range from home. Being very physically active was the norm among all my friends.

In the seventh or eighth grade, I grew interested in golf. I found some late 1940s and early 1950s golf clubs that someone was throwing out with their garbage. I chose a putter, driver, 2, 5, 7, and 9 irons, found a used collapsible canvas golf bag, and taught myself how to play golf using plastic "Wiffle" golf balls in our small yard. A "Wiffle" golf ball is a strong, hollow plastic ball with holes all over the surface. When you hit the ball, it did not travel far. In the summer I would take my clubs and walk three or four blocks to where I could catch a city bus. I could get to a city public golf course about 5 miles away with one or two transfers. The city course was 75 cents for nine holes and $1.50 for 18 for young kids.

To pay for this, I cut neighbors' lawns during the summer and school year and shoveled snow during the winter. A grass-cutting, sidewalk sweeping, and cleanup job took about two hours or so, and I would receive $2.00. This one neighbor let me use his electric grass mower with a hundred feet of electric cord following me around. This was the only neighbor who had an electric mower. When I cut other neighbors' lawns, it was with a manual push mower with a catch basket.

You may be thinking from what I have written that I was some big jock, but these activities were normal social behaviors among my friends and for many of the boys in our neighborhood. Some kids' families had a lot of money, but my family, well, we were lucky to live with my grandmother. My grandfather died when I was four years old. I was sitting in his lap while he was reading me the Sunday comics. Suddenly, he stopped reading. It looked to me like he had just fallen asleep. I got out of the chair and told my grandmother that grandpa had fallen asleep. It turns out he had passed away. Things got a little intense in the house after that. Experiencing death in person was a new event for me.

My parents had only made it through high school. Then my father went off to fight in Europe during World War II, doing extensive training here in America, then in England, then the D-day Invasion, the Battle of the Bulge, and eventually the German surrender.

Throughout my early childhood, my mother emphasized the importance of getting both a good classroom education and seeking more learning opportunities by going beyond my school studies. This included reading to learn about our country and the world around us. The nuns in grade school were great motivators for the young students. I loved studying math, history, science, and civics. With the combination of American history and civics, you learned how our government operates, and the morals, ethics, and duties that good citizenship requires.

In eighth grade, the nuns taught us how to think "outside of the box." In math, we solved problems using other base number systems besides the normal one based on the number 10. On Saturday mornings, a few of us students got together at the grade school with one of the nuns, and with her guidance, we studied and analyzed several ancient Greek plays. Besides teaching us how to become good citizens, the nuns taught us how to use "common sense" to grow wiser and become more mature. In our history classwork, the nuns explained to us how Our Founding Fathers used good morals and ethics to help form a "more perfect union."

Even with only a high school education, my mother encouraged me to read a broad range of subjects. She took me to the library every couple of weeks to get new library books to read, not only Tom Swift Jr. and The Hardy Boys, but historical books like the "We Were There" series: "We were there at Normandy, at Gettysburg," etc. As a result, even now, no matter where I go across our country, I like to visit the local library and see what it is like. Using multiple sources to create broadened learning experiences seems to expand one's mind and awareness.

During grade school, my mother taught us how to clean and maintain a home. We learned how to dust the furniture and shelves, vacuum the carpets, hand wash and dry the dishes. She taught us how to cook simple, nutritious meals in case she was not around. Grandma did the same, and we helped her with her own household chores and duties. Blue-collar dad taught us how to mow the lawn, trim the bushes, water the vegetation, wash the car, and rake the leaves in the fall. He taught us how to shoot a .22 caliber rifle, a 12 and a 20-gauge shotgun, and hunt wild rabbits and pheasant. We only hunted a couple of times, and I never had an opportunity to kill one of those animals. I later shot a .22 caliber target rifle in many high school and college match competitions.

From an early age, my father taught us self-defense, which included basic boxing and high school variations of collegiate wrestling techniques. Father excelled at wrestling in high school. He also told us a lot of stories about life on the battlefield, in foxholes, being afraid to lift your head up, and doing whatever it took just to survive. He taught me how to pay attention to the behaviors of those around me and how to not get caught up in any type of rush to judgment or knee-jerk reactions just to try and get yourself out of uncomfortable situations or harm.

Dad showed me how to make large vats of beef bone broth vegetable soup which were then put in smaller containers and placed in the long-term basement freezer. In the fall we would go past the suburbs to a farming area and buy bushels of freshly picked unhusked corn on the cob, prepare it, and freeze it for family use in the winter and following spring. Dad used the skills of his blue-collar job to do sideline remodeling work for a local butcher in exchange for a cut and wrapped quarter or half side of beef that we also kept in the freezer. Then there were the times when Walgreens would have their super ice cream sales where you could buy eight pints with the total cost being only $1.00 There were ten flavors of their house brand available. The family would divide a pint into four pieces, for an occasional dessert, one for each family member.

I grew up where the family norm was: You ate everything on your plate during meals. You did not scream, throw a tantrum, or upset the mealtime setting. My mother cooked the basics: some protein, a carbohydrate, various vegetables, and maybe a simple dessert of a couple of cookies, custard, or sometimes the treat of Grandma's homemade pound cake.

We got to know our neighbors well, at least one house deep in any direction from our home. My father told me that when he was growing up, he developed friendly relations with everyone at least 4-6 houses deep in every direction. Back then, most people often talked to their neighbors. Dad said they learned to trust you, and you got to trust them.

I never received an allowance in grade school for whatever work I did around the house. I was taught that doing household jobs just went along with the responsibilities of being a good helping family member. This principle was the same I had read numerous times in books on early American history and family life. Sharing family responsibilities was one of the qualities of family life that helped advance harmony at home and in neighborhoods.

Beginning around sixth grade, my mother started talking to me about money matters. There were very few credit cards around, and I do not remember my parents having one. We pretty much bought things using cash or a check. My mother taught me that there was a big difference between wanting something and needing something. She taught me that just because I wanted something did not mean that I should have it immediately.

I saved old silver coins back then. U.S. coin currency was mostly silver prior to 1965. My mother got me coin-collecting books where I could place coins with certain dates and mint markings. Whenever I went shopping with her and she received any change, she would let me look through her change and hunt for certain coins that might help fill in empty spaces in those coin books. We had a farmer-owned fruit and vegetable store about four blocks away, where I would sometimes walk if Mom needed something. The guy who owned it was very friendly. He wore overalls all the time and spoke in a courteous rural farming kind of way. Sometimes, I would buy a bottle of cream soda or NEHI orange soda using the money I received from grocers when I found returnable bottles lying around. You could get 2 cents for a 12-ounce glass bottle and 5 cents for the large bottles. It was amazing how many bottles you could find when you walked down alleys or went to city parks and looked in trash containers. I always checked my change from the returnable bottles to see if there were any older, dated coins before I bought my 10-cent soda.

Instead of giving me presents for my birthday or Christmas, certain relatives would give me one United States silver dollar, most with 1880 to 1925 dates. I saved all those coins and stored them at my grandmother's apartment, where she had moved after selling the house where our family had lived with her. I was far away at college when she died, and before I could get back, a distant relative of hers, who happened to have one of only two keys to her apartment, went into that apartment and stole my entire silver collection.

Though my father got to be a successful blue-collar small business owner for a while, taking good care of his few employees' incomes, he could not afford to buy his own home until 1971 when he was 50. The home cost $28,000, and his mortgage was $160 a month at 6%. His house was a small three-bedroom, one-bath brick bungalow with an unfinished basement built in the mid-1950s, with a two-car garage on a twenty-five-foot-wide lot in the city. My mother died in a car accident at 47 years old. She had a hard time with various health and genetic issues during her life.

Because of genetic issues I was born with, my college degree was in health and nutrition. I have had a life filled with many painful and traumatic experiences, some great opportunities, and numerous adventures.

Depending on your age, you may not be able to relate to what I have written about my early life as a child. No matter what your age, ask yourself if the current path most citizens are taking will result in creating positive benefits for all Americans, or is it speeding us toward some type of unstable, immoral, or unethical form of a self-destructive dystopia?

Chapter 3

CHANGING PATHS: DASHING THROUGH LIFE

How did Americans prior to the 1950s make decisions about their lives before television, the internet, smartphones, and electronic social media told them what to wear, how to act, what to buy, and how to raise their children? For a couple of hundred years here in America, citizens used their minds to figure out their paths, their priorities, and their purchases without some form of technological visualization and electronic communication giving them "screen" advice to guide them on their journey.

During our lives, we are faced with alternative paths or choices. As a young child, we can touch that hot stove and burn our hands or do what mommy says and not touch it. We can get into places that will cause us harm, or we can remember what Daddy said: "Don't go in or near that place, you could get hurt." Some children heeded the advice; others often suffered severe consequences.

As a teenager, life gets trickier. The variety of friends we experience may become more diverse and more frequent with the possibility of encountering "bad apples" who had misdirected childhoods or no positive parental input. In some situations, extreme negative youth behaviors can be experienced by both poor, oppressed children or rich, spoiled youths.

As a teen, we can encounter fellow students or friends who smoke cigarettes, drink alcohol, and use illegal drugs, and we can choose to join them, or we can choose a different path without these behaviors. In our teens and 20s, people can date others who are "easy to get in the sack," or we can choose companions who aren't easy but who are compatible with us morally and emotionally. Maybe our choices have a desire to become more compatible in a wider range of subjects, activities, and goals.

Life is a journey of self-discovery. If you take your time and do not rush from one adventure to another without "digesting" or understanding these episodes in your head and heart, your path may be a little slower but more stable and fulfilling.

If you lived in the 1960s, you heard many songs about love and "being happy together." You also had other avenues to expand your consciousness and perception through physical movement, Eastern philosophies, healthy eating, being a "flower child," or even sitting on a mountain-top and clearing your mind through meditation. There were hippie movements, using concepts like "working together for the common good," "give peace a chance," and "all you need is love," which became common. Maybe you were influenced by sayings from well-known people:

"Never doubt that a small group of thoughtful, committed individuals can change the world, it's the only thing that ever has."

- Margaret Meade

"He who takes a stand is often wrong, but he who fails to take a stand is always wrong."

- Anonymous

"You're either on the bus or off the bus."

-Ken Kesey

"Be Here Now."

-Ram Dass

"It all depends on how we look at things, and not how they are in themselves."
-Carl Jung

"Always trust those who are searching for the truth, never those who have found it."

-Jordan Maxwell

"To gain that which is worth having, it may be necessary to lose everything else."

-Bernadette Devlin

"Follow your bliss and the universe will open doors where there were only walls."

-Joseph Campbell

Some paths lead to pain; others lead to healing. We all choose different roads that we encounter on our life-long journey. No one shoveled those questionable foods into your mouth that caught up with you later in life. No one stopped you from exercising or getting a good night's sleep. No one forced you to marry the person of your choice unless you got someone pregnant or became pregnant yourself. Maybe in that job you chose, you were making "good bucks," but the strains of the job were making you sick, depressed, or angry. Maybe with that extra income you were receiving, you could spoil your kids and wife, maybe even yourself, with excessive materialism. Do you voice comments to friends or family like these? "I've got to get the latest smartphones for everyone in the family to be happy." "Why take the time to cook something healthy when I can just get some premade pizzas or fried chicken with lots of soda for the family on the way home from work, along with a couple of bottles of that new chardonnay or Merlot that Bill and I talked about?" "Forget junior college or a state school. Our kids deserve the best. We'll just take out some student loans for them, and they can get a college degree from a quality school." "Time to go on another family vacation to someplace memorable to break away from the monotony around us here, maybe a nice fancy resort where we will be catered to like we deserve."

Here is a short story, often the aftermath of a lifestyle I just described.

"What the fu--! You're dropping out of college after two years? Are you flunking out? You said you were doing well. Yes, I know your sister dropped out last year, but she got pregnant and had to marry that low life she was involved with.

At least you can't get pregnant. Wait. Is your girlfriend pregnant?

No, huh. Well, what happened?

Two DWIs, speeding, and you smashed into another car?

Your fault, and the judge said a short jail time and a big fine, plus expenses? I don't have that kind of money available right now, I would have to liquidate some of my 401k or something.

NO. I am not selling the new BMW; I just got it recently with big monthly payments.

OK, son, I'll figure something out.

Your mother? She's seeing a therapist, no, I don't want to talk about it!

(Five years later)

What, another child, isn't that your third or fourth? (I think I need another drink.) Yes, you will always be my little girl, I'll send something this week. Your brother? It's been five years since I've heard from him. I don't even know where he is. Stopped communicating with me when I refused to keep sending him more and more money. Mom? She just filed for a divorce last week and wants half of everything except the bills. Me? Doc says heart disease and ulcers. Yes, I stopped smoking. Thanks, sweetie pie. Good luck to you, too.

(Ten years later)

You're downsizing and you're firing me? I've been loyal to this company all these years. I'm in a tough situation, I had to sell the house after the divorce, and my 401k is almost empty. Hell, I'm 63. I'll have to take early Social Security and try to find another job. Who wants to hire an overweight, stressed-out, almost-broke 63-year-old?

(Three years later)

Ring, ring, ring. Oh, so nice to hear from you. Yes, you're still my little girl. Yes, I'm back in the hospital, a second heart attack, doc said next one might be it. My little apartment is fine. I'm getting by. Your brother? No idea. Thinking about it just gets me closer to the grave. Mom? Married some millionaire on Marco Island in Florida. She loved flaunting her cleavage. Heard about her from one of her friends I ran into at the grocery store a couple of months ago. Bye, honey.

(One year later)

He was only 67. Looks a lot older lying in that casket. That's the daughter over there. She's the only family member that showed up. How did he die? They found him in his apartment, slumped over on his kitchen table, with his face sitting on a plate of barbeque ribs. His heart just exploded, I guess, but the glass of wine next to the ribs didn't spill."

We all have historical stories of our individual and shared family lives. Some people are born into great wealth where every opportunity for success is provided for them, yet they become abusive alcoholics and/or drug addicts. Another person may be born into extreme poverty where every step forward in their life is met with sorrow and adversity, yet they overcome the hardships, decide to work harder, and become more focused on being a moral and honest person who looks out for others besides themselves. They may not become multimillionaires, but as senior citizens, they can reflect on their many years of helping others, staying true to their moral compass, and being appreciative of life in general.

OLD WAYS DON'T DIE

When I talk to people and say that maybe society should be looking at certain positive human behaviors and philosophical beliefs that occurred fifty to seventy years ago to try and solve many of today's social dilemmas, I often hear this response: "Times have changed too much to go back and find solutions to today's problems." Really?

Today, many people believe that technology clarifies and amplifies their lives. They claim it can solve their problems because now they have access to unlimited information on the Internet. Others say technology provides them with music that either calms their stress or distracts their focus away from their problems for a short period of time. Some people even say that the little voice-activated box on their desk will answer all their questions about anything. Politicians can use the Internet to expand their methods of lies and propaganda to persuade even more people that you should vote for them instead of anyone else. By using X (Tweets) or texts, for example, politicians can voice their opinions, biases, and prejudices without speaking orally to the voters to answer questions about what their legislative pronouncements and policies mean for their voters. In other words, they control the conversation without having to respond.

Why is there so much emphasis on forgetting or ignoring historically proven advice about etiquette, honesty, morality, and ethical behaviors in both politics and business activities? Is it because, with today's focus on tribalism, everything in your political, social, or economic life needs to be valued using a tribal interpretation? Or maybe it's greed.

In my research, I have come across several interesting observations made by various people that may be very relevant to what is occurring in America today, and I would like to share some of them with you here.

"On the internet, a person could spend a lifetime in egomaniacal self-worship…seeking the truth is no longer fashionable, living reality TV lives is more entertaining. The only real truth is doing whatever is necessary to get whatever we want to please ourselves…people are addicted to being right."[7] (Chuck Palahniuk)

"All privilege based on wealth, and all enmity to honest men merely because they are wealthy are un-American – both of them equally so. The things that will destroy America are prosperity-at-any-price, the love of soft living, and the get-rich-quick theory of life."[8] (Theodore Roosevelt)

"The example of great and pure personages is the only thing that can lead us to fine ideas and noble deeds. Money only appeals to selfishness and always irresistibly tempts its owners to abuse it."[9] (Albert Einstein)

"The smartphone is the modern-day hypodermic needle, delivering digital dopamine 24/7 for a wired generation. If you haven't met your drug of choice yet, it's coming soon to a website near you." (Dr. Anna Lembke, medical director of Stanford Addiction Medicine in her book "Dopamine Nation.")

A lot of personal relations today use technology to interact and communicate with each other. This reminds me of terminology that was used years ago by the cartoon character Homer Simpson. I say this because today, technology seems to be more like a god with its own set of beliefs and values. If you look at technology's mantra that claims, "Our advances every day will make your life easier, you will be more connected to everyone and everything, and we will provide your ultimate solutions," it reminds me of that Homer Simpson quote. I revised it by changing one word to make it appropriate for today. "Technology, the cause of and solution to all of life's problems."[10]

THE CHANGING SOCIETY

American society has been rapidly changing in the last couple of decades, especially with technological devices now consuming more and more of our time and energy. These devices seem to be degrading our ability to naturally rationalize our behavior. It doesn't seem like we are trying to achieve a more balanced outlook and approach in how we deal with our everyday life choices. Degradation does not appear to be a concern for those individuals who enjoy the highly amplified emotional, psychological, and physical lifestyles and mannerisms now exhibited in society. Some of you may be wondering: "What is he talking about?"

I am talking about the cultural shift away from social mores, cultural decencies, and ethical behaviors: those historical virtues that have been with us for thousands of years. Here are some examples.

"Companies didn't have to consider the welfare of workers on par with stockholders. Couples didn't have to be in committed relationships to have sex or be married to have children. Children didn't have to care for elderly parents. There were a million 'have tos' to argue about. But the cumulative effect was an erosion of socially shared ways of treating others respectfully, the ties that make community possible. A new selfism trumped everyday moral impulses."[11] (Dick Meyer)

What you are seeing today in our culture is the result of the many changed perspectives that have developed from an "only me selfism" that is in direct contrast to the traditional "we are a community of caring citizens" approach that originally built our country.

"Our rules have become fluid, weak, and relativistic in parts of life as different as entertainment, etiquette, and ethics…It creates friction, which rubs and burns and makes us cranky...Increasingly, Americans live without deeper forms of what we casually call 'support networks' that help and nourish us, both practically and emotionally. World views or 'ready guides' came primarily from community, teaching, and example, not from the Internet and journeys of self-discover…It is as if our plenty (wealth) has freed us to act out and behave poorly. We have the extra time and safety to invent all sorts of head problems."[12] (Meyer)

What do many people believe today? Remember what George Costanza said on the TV show "Seinfeld": "Jerry, just remember, it's not a lie if you believe it."

"You can pick the facts and concepts you wish to be true...In a perversion of classic American ideals, picking what truth to believe in is now considered a basic right, the very thing individuals ought to do if they are making their own free, honest choices and creating their authentic identities. Objective truth is medieval."[13] (Meyer)

Why go medieval when you can have "truthiness" instead? Webster's Dictionary defines Truthiness as: "truth that comes from the gut, not books" and "the quality of preferring concepts or facts one wishes to be true, rather than concepts and facts known to be true."

Why become a full-fledged adult when you can stay a child? Charles Chaput, the Roman Catholic Archbishop of Denver, Colorado, from 1997-2011, and Archbishop of Philadelphia from 2011-2020, once said this about becoming an adult: "Much of American culture right now is built on an adolescent fiction. The fiction is that life is all about you as an individual, your ideals, your appetite, and your needs. It isn't. Adulthood brings power. Power brings responsibility. And the meaning of your life will hinge on simple, basic choices. Will you engage the world with your heart and brains and faith, and work to make it a better place – not just for yourself and the people you love but also for people you don't even know whose survival depends on your service to the common good? Or will you wrap yourself in a blanket of noise and toys and consumer junk and stay a child?"[14]

Are you thinking that what I am talking about comes from a Liberal perspective? How about reading and paying attention to the words of a true Conservative, Jonah Jacob Goldberg, an American Conservative syndicated columnist, author, political analyst, and commentator. From 1998 until May 2019, he was an editor at the "National Review."

"Popular culture, with its emphasis on hedonism, animism, or just simple feeling, is the primary public conveyor of meaning in our lives, and it's with few exceptions, unattached from (and often hostile to) higher understandings of meaning, morality, or religion…we are becoming what we worship, and what we worship is ourselves…Our feelings have become an end in themselves. How we feel – not what we conclude – is the higher truth…Giving in to the passion of the crowd is inherently corrupting, because it seeks no higher authority than itself and says you have a righteous entitlement to act on your gut.

"But the culture of feeling…creates a mind-set, an orientation, a sense of entitlement about how the world around us is supposed to unfold…This desire for the hero to win, regardless of whether the victory is objectively desirable, is not merely romantic. It is also tribal. It says that my team must triumph, our will must be satisfied, and all impediments are equally illegitimate."[15]

What he is talking about can best be seen in many of the political rallies of United States politicians who preach that "they are in the right and any opposition is wrong." They go beyond this and say that not only is the opposition wrong, but they are evil, corrupt, and have no place in our society. "This tribal us-versus-them worldview is intensified on social media where it is easier to find like-minded but virtual 'friends' a thousand miles away than it is to have a conversation with your actual neighbor…When one of my people suffers, I feel pain. When 'the other' suffers, I take delight."[16] (Goldberg)

Could a lot of what is happening in our culture have anything to do with parenting, how children are raised, or how adults have become the new children in our society? Thirty or so years ago, Neil Postman wrote in "Amusing Ourselves to Death: Public Discourse in the Age of Show Business" that childhood fully bloomed around 1850 but started a rapid decline around 1950. What he wrote was mainly about America's white culture. Then, in his work "The Disappearance of Childhood," Postman said that it was admirable that society saw fit to get the children out of the factories at young ages in the 1800s and to help children adjust to society by going from child coziness to tough love. But around 1950, things changed.

The disappearance of childhood is traceable directly, he says, to the rise of electronic media. "What separated childhood from adulthood previously was a secret or guarded knowledge about full adult reality that was understandable only by literacy…Television changed all that because it is a 'total disclosure medium,' operating around the clock, demanding and broadcasting a nonstop supply of new and titillating information. Practically nothing is taboo or off-limits. Because television doesn't know or care who's watching, the medium effectively 'adultifies' children while infantilizing adults. We are left with a nation not only of childish adults but also of adult children…Everywhere one looks, the behavior, language, attitudes, and desires – even the physical appearance of adults and children is becoming increasingly indistinguishable."[17]

Republican United States Senator Ben Sass, in his book "The Vanishing American Adult," translates psychologist Jeffery Jenson Arnett's term "emerging adulthood." "It's a rich nation problem. The more affluent the society, the more likely young people will experience an extended drift toward adulthood. Wealthy societies, for reasons largely well-intentioned but now producing unintended consequences, are making it easier for their teens to avoid the rigors and responsibilities of becoming a grown-up."[18] Psychologist Jeffery Arnett calls those years the "self-focused age," when there are few real responsibilities, few "daily obligations," and limited "commitments to others." In a state when young people were once supposed to learn to "stand alone as a self-sufficient person, they find themselves increasingly paralyzed by over-choice."[19]

"Notre Dame sociologist Christian Smith and his team…found a dark underbelly to this 'fun and freedom' of early adulthood. For most young people, this boundlessness is experienced as a kind of loneliness. The dominant feelings are not hope but 'personal struggle, confusion, anxiety, hurt, frustration, and grief.' Many of these young people sense that they are morally adrift, 'captive to consumerism,' chasing pleasure through binge drinking and casual hookups, and disengaged civically and politically."[20] (Sasse)

The following is part of a letter written to a help columnist in a publication called "The Daily Mail" from a mother concerning her children and her family.

"I see children who lack restraint almost daily – and they are my own. What's more, my husband and I are to blame. Instead of teaching our children discipline and boundaries, we, like many modern middle-class parents, have tried to reason with them instead. My children don't spend hours playing online, but they don't get a lot of time to wind down. Imogen started ballet when she was three and now learns swimming, gymnastics, and piano. Hugo is about to start football, which we'll fit around music class.

Even Oscar goes to baby yoga and sing-along drop-in. My husband goes away for work a lot. So, we have been unavailable for long periods of time when our children need us. Instead, they've been brought up by a succession of kind but professional childcare experts – nannies and au pairs. We bought into the notion that children are mini adults with rational minds, able to understand arguments and make considered decisions." (Factual statement concerning this letter: as of the day the woman wrote and submitted the letter to "The Daily Mail," Imogen was 5, Hugo was 4, and Oscar was two years old.)[21]

Dr. Leonard Sax, a Pennsylvania family physician and psychologist well known for writing about children's development, has stated that the role of parenting has collapsed, and all too often, adults defer decisions to their children because the parents have relinquished parental authority and lost confidence in themselves.

In Sax's book, "The Collapse of Parenting: How We Hurt Our Kids When We Treat Them Like Grown-ups," he says, "A functional family unit hinges on the one social construct that contemporary society has been working hard to dismantle: hierarchy."

In his book, "The Intuitive Parent: Why the Best Thing for Your Child Is You," Stephen Camarata, Professor of Hearing and Speech Sciences and Psychiatry at Vanderbilt University in Nashville, Tennessee, writes that "this idea of pushing your children to the absolute max of their development norm doesn't give them time to reason and problem solve. It actually undermines both self-confidence and fluid reasoning or the ability to think…We're treating them like little hard drives."

A great influence on children is what the child picks up from his/her same-age peers, which competes with the guidance they receive from their parents. "Kids are not born knowing right from wrong," says Dr. Leonard Sax, referring to many studies reporting that children left on their own to decipher right from wrong have more negative outcomes later in life. "That child in their late 20s is much more likely to be anxious, depressed, less likely to be gainfully employed, less likely to be healthy, more likely to be addicted to drugs or alcohol. Parents who are authoritative have better outcomes, and it's a larger effect than the effect of race, ethnicity, household income, or IQ."[22] [23]

In a parent's desire to provide their children with more physical possessions and social activities, have they lost sight of the historically important behavior of being an inspirational example for their children to follow?

When a parent presents a wholesome, positive example, children will learn the moral and ethical differences between right and wrong. If you do not teach them yourselves with established rules and guidelines that are reinforced daily, they will learn and adopt the values of their friends and the "anything and everything is acceptable" internet.

Chapter 4

BEHAVIORAL ADDICTIONS: OUR BEST FRIENDS

We are a country fixated-on behavioral addictions, and we are not going to stop having an addictive culture until something very intense wakes us up. Maybe for some people, COVID-19 was the start of the solution to help change their behavior. But there are too many powerful corporate and political forces that do not want behavior addictions in America to stop. Are you thinking that I am a doomsday person or an extremist? When Covid first started, no one believed those so-called extremist scientists that were predicting that at least 1 million people would die from the Pandemic. Over 1.1 million people in the United States did die.

True extremism is evident in our daily social behaviors toward ourselves and our fellow citizens. Most people, when they hear the words "addict, addiction, or addictive behavior," think of the person in the alley with a syringe in their arm, shooting heroin or meth, or someone constantly snorting cocaine to try and keep the "high."

Some people might categorize addictive behavior as being connected to alcoholism: the Skid Row bum in the gutters, dressed in tatters, unshaven, ratty hair, directionless in their lives. No one wants to be compared to a heroin junkie or an alcoholic sleeping in the alley. These alcoholics and drug junkies are just a small portion of this country's true addictive behaviorists; they are peoples' scapegoats to justify pointing a finger at someone else instead of themselves. As a culture, we are rarely willing to admit that our daily behavioral addictions are harmful to us. All addictive behaviors have personal consequences for us, our families, our friends, and our nation, whether you want to accept it or not.

Our culture distorts the perception of reality by allowing escapism and extremism to flourish. We voice an acceptance of most addictive activities as socially normal, legal behaviors. Maybe we rationalize the behaviors as acceptable because many of our friends are doing the same things, and we do not want to be left out or seen as loners. People say: "Why change? We are just like everyone else we know."

People don't quickly develop addictive behaviors like someone might from shooting meth or heroin, where the first impact is so intense or seductive that the effect overwhelms you with whatever type of ultimate pleasure the substance can produce. Most socially addictive behaviors develop over time, usually through encouragement from friends, parents, peers, or the thousands of advertisements on our screens.

"Honey, I just needed a couple of highballs after work today to take the edge off my day. Hey, can we open that new bottle of wine I got for tonight's dinner? Don't worry, that prescription I got from the doctor will get me going in the morning, along with a couple of cups of coffee."

"So, what's the big deal? We finished off two or three bottles of that good wine with our friends Jim and Jill. They are our best friends. What are friends for?"

If your normal everyday behaviors interfere with your health, well-being, financial status, education, relationships, or sleep, don't you think that maybe you are over-participating in addictive behaviors? Maybe you need to do something about them. But who cares? The government surely does not care, and maybe your friends don't care either, but your choices in life should not generally be decided by your friends, parents, the government, or the advertisements seen through media access.

Maybe you want to grow up to be like your parents. A parent is one of the primary examples that a child has in their life to follow. What if your father is a verbally abusive, alcoholic, obese person, or your mother is satisfied with just giving her children money or gifts instead of taking the time to listen to what is on their minds and talk to them about problems they may be having in school or with a friend?

Therapists often hear children say something like this: "Gee, if it wasn't for all the pills she takes, or all the wine she drinks, or all the social events she attends, then add her busy job, which takes up most of her time and energy, when does she have time to be my real mother?"

Have you ever watched the old TV programs "Father Knows Best" and "Leave it to Beaver?" On these 1950s-60s TV shows, we saw children's problems discussed calmly in their bedrooms or at the dinner table. As a parent, are you setting a good example for your children and grandchildren to follow by your behavior toward them? How do you feel when you see your children mimicking your bad, addictive behaviors? They then may use these same attitudes toward others, including you, their parents.

Do you think that maybe there could be some type of role that the government could play in trying to change the amount of addictive behavior that goes on in our country? If you were to study this addictive behavior problem, you would find just the opposite to be true.

The Federal, state, and many local governmental representatives in America accept people who have both legal and illegal behavioral addictions. The treatment of addictive behaviors is often funded by taxes, which employ a lot of professional workers: judges and the whole court system, lawyers, multiple types of therapists or counselors, police departments, jails, medical personnel, and addictive behavioral centers, to name a few of the employed jobs. With the number of addictive behaviors increasing, they also create greater profits for the companies who manufacture the addictive products, and these profits fill the pocketbooks of companies and stockholders. Just look at how the recent opioid crisis has benefited the economics of pharmaceutical companies, medical treatment personnel, police departments, hospitals, doctors, EMTs, etc.

To understand the problem with addictive behaviors, you need to look beyond legal and illegal drug addiction. Let's start with a simple definition and proceed from there. Oxford Dictionary defines addiction as "the fact or condition of being addicted to a particular substance, thing, or activity." Now let us get into more detail.

The American Society of Addictive Medicine defines addiction as: "a primary chronic disease of brain reward, motivation, memory, and related circuitry…characterized by inability to consistently abstain, impairment in behavioral control, craving, diminished recognition of significant problems with one's behaviors and interpersonal relationships, and a dysfunctional emotional response."[24] This is the simplistic version, and if you want to understand the complete picture, check out the reference.

There are many types of legal and illegal addictions. I would like to mention one legal addiction that is dominant in America and the many consequences of its behavior.

OBESITY

In most cases, obesity is a self-induced disease. The word "disease" in social networks of communication has become an escapist terminology to medically categorize and justify its treatment by both the Federal Government and insurance companies. Years ago, the rate of obesity was low. Go back and look at photos of your own family members from 1940 to 1970. After this time frame, the percentage of obese people started climbing. After the year 2000, the obesity rates really accelerated higher.

In 2013, the American Medical Association came out and classified obesity as a disease. This spurred doctors, psychologists, and medical insurers to see this overeating problem as a monetary gold-mining opportunity. I sum it up this way: "If you want to eat as much as you want of high fat, high sugar, high salt, high protein, and carbohydrate foods, don't worry because we will get paid by some entity for treating you. This is America, land of the free-to-eat all and anything you want no matter what the consequences might be to yourself, your family, or the nation."

Did you know that the American Medical Association's own Council on Science and Public Health was against classifying obesity as a disease? Was this an example of money and political power not listening to science like we often experienced with COVID-19? This sounds like another example where fostering a culture of personal responsibility falls by the wayside when those in power control the messaging to the public.

Obesity does not come from the air we breathe, the water we drink, an infected cut, or an obesity germ that some people get when someone coughs in their direction. Obesity occurs when a person repeatedly puts excessive amounts of solid or liquid food in their mouth and swallows it. No one is putting a gun to your head, demanding that you eat a 3000-calorie Super Monster Triple Decker Beef Burger with double cheese, exotic dressing, a large order of Cheese Fries, and a 32-ounce soft drink for lunch. If your mother bought you this for your lunch when you were 10-16 years old, she should have been arrested for child abuse.

So here are some thought-provoking philosophical questions.

How can obese people claim to be environmentalists or conservatives when they consume excessive amounts of food, use excessive material for clothing (often made of synthetic fabrics made from crude oil), and over-use medical facilities and professionals? Then there are the costs of materials from natural and synthetic resources to build bigger chairs and tables to accommodate the extra weight. People can get so large and out of shape that they can no longer help people in their presence who may need immediate help or even be able to help themselves in an emergency. Obese people can get to the point where they can no longer work and must depend on the government for aid and assistance. What kind of an example are obese people giving to their children who look to their parents for guidance about how they should eat to stay healthy?

Another aspect of obesity has come to my attention. A study in 2018 from the Council for a Strong America, called "Unhealthy and Unprepared," said that almost one-third of young Americans are too overweight to join the military. They state that: "Obesity has long threatened our nation's health. As the epidemic grows, obesity is posing a threat to our nation's security as well." The United States Department of Defense states that 71% of Americans between the ages of 17-24 do not meet the sign-up standards. The report was compiled by a group of retired generals and admirals. "Basic training lasts weeks, but building strong troops takes years. Encouraging healthy lifestyles early in life will help our nation prepare for future challenges," retired Air Force General Richard Meyers said.[25]

The report concludes that both parents and children need to focus early in life on healthy eating and lifestyles, and the importance of positive physical activities from the time the children are young. We are seeing a lot of negative influences in the public domain that are affecting our children, especially through the internet, but very few positive ones concerning their mental and physical health.

Obese people can marry other obese people. Children often look at their parents as examples of how they should live, how they eat, how they are inactive, or how their parents might not seem to care about their health. Not being good examples for your children who also become obese helps foster future generations with altered genetics and hormonal imbalances, which will create serious health issues. It's called "epigenetic inheritance." Many people may take offense at this next statement, but it is true. Farmers and agricultural scientists do not produce large animals that eventually wind up on your dinner plate by breeding skinny animals. Over generations, families can also genetically alter their body size to be larger.

Have you ever watched The Learning Channel on TV? Try watching the programs "My 600 Pound Life," "Too Big," or "1000 Pound Best Friends" if you want to see how obesity affects the lives of the obese, their children, and family. There may be other similar programs available. Obese people develop much higher occurrences of serious health problems, but people on their journey to obesity do not want to accept this.

A report from the New England Journal of Medicine has recently been published that analyzed data from six million Americans. "If America does not collectively adopt healthier eating habits, over half of the nation will be obese within ten years. Even worse, one in four Americans will be 'severely obese' with a body mass index over 35, which means they will be more than 100 pounds overweight." The current obesity rate in Louisiana, Oklahoma, and West Virginia is over 40%.

"The societal cost is high," said Aviva Must, chair of Tufts University Public Health and Community Medicine, "both in terms of obesity-related health consequences and healthcare expenditures which could bring us to our knees. 50 years ago, obesity was a relatively rare condition. People who were poor were underweight, not overweight, but that has changed…one reason is the rise of sugar, sweetened beverages, and ultra-processed food, which contribute calories but little nutrition."[26]

Does all this public and private research concerning the consequences of being obese have any effect on your own personal outlook or on the health outcome of your children? Maybe you just label it as fake news, left-wing propaganda, but if you are 55-65 in a hospital bed dying of heart disease you may be rethinking your attitude.

THE QUEEN OF CONSUMPTION

Have you ever heard of a woman named Molly Schuyler? At a competitive eating contest in Clarence, New York, in the fall of 2018, she ate 44 plates of pumpkin pie in 10 minutes at the Great Pumpkin Farm. That was about the same as eating 5.5 whole pies. She is reported to hold the world records for the consumption of pizza, bratwurst, hamburgers, and other foods, including eating a 72-ounce steak in 3 minutes. So, what is her secret? She does not chew.

There is a Major League Eating organization that holds a series of eating contests that are supervised and regulated by the International Federation of Competitive Eating. This was a new venture that started in 1997. One of the famous contests held by this organization is Nathan's Hot Dog Eating Contest held every Fourth of July at Coney Island in Brooklyn, New York City. Though Molly does not belong to this organization, she may be the world's best volume and speed eater.

These eating events staged in both the United States and Canada draw large numbers of fans. Pigging out on food is very popular. Is it any wonder that more and more people are becoming obese? When overeating is sanctioned around the country by these events, is it not surprising that ordinary people have contests among themselves about who can consume the greatest amount of a chosen food?

There is a program on television called "Man Versus Food" that is on the Travel Channel and the Cooking Channel, which has the host travel to various restaurants around the country. He competes in time challenges to eat a "special house meal" in an allotted time frame. The many pounds of food, special house challenge is available to anyone who visits the restaurant. Before competing in a house special challenge, the show host samples menus from nearby restaurants. During the time that the host is trying to consume the massive, eat everything challenge within a certain allotted time, both the visiting crowd and restaurant workers are chanting and wildly screaming encouragements to the show host before his time runs out. If the host finishes the meal within the time limit, he is rewarded with a printed T-shirt and has his picture taken to be put on the restaurant's Hall of Fame wall display for those who have successfully finished the challenge. Lots of average people try to complete these challenges at numerous restaurants around the country.

I would like to give you some food statistics concerning Nathan's Famous Hot Dog Eating Contest, which was won by Joey Chestnut for the 16th time in 2023. He's only lost once in this contest since he started competing in 2007. In 2020, for example, Mr. Chestnut ate 75 hot dogs and 75 hot dog buns in 10 minutes. Here are the statistics of what he ate:

Calories	21,000
Grams of Fat	1078.5
Mg of sodium	51,000
Grams of carbs	1875
Grams of Sugar	225
Grams of Protein	675 [27]

The following is a list of the greatest number of specific foods that a person has eaten in an allotted time frame compiled by the Major League Eating Organization as of January 2020. These statistics have barely changed since then. I picked categories most people can relate to in their normal eating practices. Thousands of fans from all over the country attend these contests, and many develop volume eating techniques to qualify for these events. Competitive eating may provide psychological inducements for overeating food, which can lead to obesity.

Butter – 7 quarter pound sticks, salted butter in 5 minutes.

Buffalo wild chicken wings- 7.61 lbs. in 12 min.

Chili – 2.438 gallons in 6 min.

Eggs – 141 hard-boiled in 8 min.

Glazed donuts – 59.5 in 8 min.

Pancakes – 50 3.25 oz. Wild Eggs Pancakes in 10 min.

Mayonnaise – four 32 oz. bowls in 8 min.

Shrimp - 4 lbs. 15 oz. spot shrimp in 12 min.

Sweet corn – 61.75 ears in 12 min.

Pasta – 10 lbs. spaghetti and red sauce in 8 min.

Cheesecake – 11 lbs. Downtown Atlanta in 9 min.

Candy bars – 2 lbs. chocolate bars in 6 min.

Baked beans –10 lbs. in 1 min. 45 sec.

Spam – 9.75 lbs. from the can in 8 min.

Grilled cheese sandwiches – 47 in 10 min.

Tamales – 102 in 12 min.

Ice cream, short form – 16.5 pints of vanilla in 6 min.

Peanut butter and jelly sandwiches – 42 in 10 min.

Nigiri sushi – 141 pieces in 6 min.

Rocky Mountain Oysters (bull's testicles)– 3 lbs. 11.75 oz. in 10 min.

Cupcakes – 72 in 6 min.

Apple pie – 4.375 three-pound pies in 10 min.

Twinkies – 121 in 6 min.

Bacon – 182 strips of Smithfield Bacon in 5 min.

Taco Bell Tacos – 53 soft beef tacos in 10 min.

Corned beef sandwiches – 20 8 ounce in 12 min.

Philly cheesesteaks – 23 6" sandwiches in 10 min.

French Fries – 4.46 lbs. Nathan's Famous Crinkle in 6 min.

Popcorn – 28 5.24oz. servings in 8 minutes

Are you starting to feel full? Or do you need another serving?

YOU ARE WHAT YOU EAT

"Think healthy, eat sparingly, exercise regularly, walk a lot, and think positively about yourself." (Norman Vincent Peale)

There was a phrase that was popular during the 1960s/1970s concerning how people chose the foods that they ate. Many people thought that the phrase was just another aspect of the hippie/new age movement, along with other phrases like Timothy Leary's "Turn on, tune in, and drop out." The food phrase was: "You are what you eat."

During the 1950s and 1960s, we saw the rugged cowboy image portrayed in shows like Wagon Train, Gunsmoke, and Rawhide. If you watched these shows, you got the "cleaned up" version of what life was really like in the 1800s. The TV audiences were mostly families, so the more realistic 2004-06 HBO "Deadwood" TV series life portrayals of the 1870s were not allowed to be shown. Beer, whiskey, steak, pinto beans, biscuits, eggs, and pie with strong black coffee were portrayed as food mainstays. A cowboy's real life on the range was much different.

Remember the Marlboro Man commercials from 1968 to 1989. An amazing fact about that person in real life was that he never smoked cigarettes, but the sale of cigarettes was huge back then. Even the cartoon character Fred Flintstone smoked Winston cigarettes in TV ads. Smoking, drinking alcohol, and eating steaks made you a man; at least, that was what advertisers tried to tell you.

Then along came the Hippie and New Age Movements with a new perspective on eating with the slogan: "You are what you eat." Many people rejected the phrase, thinking that "if it came from these long-haired hippies, it was un-American." The phrase "you are what you eat" may have begun in France in 1826 when French physician Anthelme Brillat-Savarin wrote, "Tell me what you eat, and I will tell you what you are." Then, in the 1800s, Mr. Kellogg and Mr. Post preached healthy eating and the benefits of their new breakfast cereals and foods. Dr. Kellogg started his Battle Creek, Michigan Sanitarium health resort in 1876. At the time, the word "sanatorium" meant a health resort for invalid soldiers. Kellogg changed the second "a" in the word to an "i" and the "o" to an "a" in naming the resort complex. This was around 1877-78.

Over time, people from all over the world came to "be healed" or to recuperate using Kellogg's practices of healthy eating, mental and physical therapies, and recreation. (In 1993, T. Coraghessan Boyle wrote a book called "The Road to Wellville" about the sanitarium that John Harvey Kellogg built in Michigan. In 1994, a movie with the same name came out about this Battle Creek institution and Dr. Kellogg. The book showed a more serious description, and the movie showed many comical portrayals of Kellogg's work.)

The history of Dr. Kellogg and his family is extensively covered in a book called: "The Kelloggs: The Battling Brothers of Battle Creek."[28] This is a fascinating description of not only the Kellogg family but of the early years of the breakfast food business in general. For decades, the breakfast cereal business in the United States sold many whole grain cereals to families looking for easy, short preparation time breakfasts. At one point, Battle Creek was home to dozens of breakfast cereal companies. After the Kellogg brothers died, others less dedicated to health took over the company. Sugar and other non-natural products started being added to the cereals.

The 1950s and 1960s saw the introduction of high amounts of sugars and flavorings. Coco Puffs, Lucky Charms, Frosty O's, Trix, Fruit Loops, and Kreme Krunch-Vanilla/Orange/Strawberry were nothing like Wheaties, Shredded Wheat, Corn Flakes, or Bran Flakes. The addition of sugar made the cereals taste more like candy, and the youth of America went wild consuming these new flavored cereals. For example, one serving (3/4 of a cup) of Fruit Loops had 12.9 grams of sugar, 1.1 grams of fat, and 1.1 grams of protein. Some generics of this cereal have up to 21 grams of sugar per serving. But how many adults or children eat only ¾ of a cup of cereal? In the list of ingredients, it shows that there is more sugar than any other component. The product also has no fruit, but it does have synthetic dyes red 40, blue 2, yellow 6, and blue 1. In comparison, Shredded Wheat has 0 sugars, 1 gram of fat, and 5 grams of protein, and it is made of whole grain wheat.

There was another health nutritionist who was active in the early 1900s. His name was Victor Lindlahr. He wrote that 90% of the diseases known to man are caused by cheap foodstuffs - you are what you eat. He had a radio program (1936-1953) that reached millions of listeners, proclaiming the benefits of good nutrition. His 1942 book was called: "You Are What You Eat: How to Win and Keep Health with Diet." So, the Hippie/New Age movement of the 1960s and 1970s was just revisiting the policies and practices advocated by Brillat-Savarin, Kellogg, Lindlahr, and others. Something old was once again something new or with a different perspective. This common-sense approach toward healthy eating keeps reappearing in our history. But are most people paying attention?

Repeatedly in the last 150 years, Americans have been informed by various holistic health professionals that maybe it is time to wake up and open their minds to eating more natural foods and exercising their bodies. Getting the right amount of sleep also benefits your health.

There is a simple test you can do for a self-health evaluation. Just before you get into a shower or bathtub, look at yourself in a full-length mirror. Ask yourself: is this the best I can do? Are you proud of what you are seeing? What you see in that mirror is what you have created from what you are eating and what little exercise you are doing. We live in America, not North Korea. No one is forcing you to put massive amounts of food calories into your mouth by holding a gun to your head.

Another food factor that seems to be popular today is the additional flavors people add to the foods they eat to enhance their taste. Have you ever watched the program "Chopped" on the Food Network? This program, and several others like it that satisfy your flavor cravings are extremely popular among all ages starting around age eight or so. Many of the judges who rate the meals that contestants prepare are not excellent examples of good health. That fact alone might tell you something about what the judges may favor in foods. These judges want the contestants to really crank up the flavors to be acceptable to their judging palates. Finished food dishes can't be soothing, mellow, too healthy, or mildly satisfying. They need to be rich, intense, not too mild or too hot and spicy, dynamic, unique, look pleasing on the plate, tender, full-bodied, not too oily, not too bland, creative, etc. If you do not meet the judges' standards, you are "chopped" (eliminated) from the competition. The carryover for those who watch these programs might be an expectational standard of what a cook at home should use in their own family food preparation. Common sense food preparation based on preparing a meal with balanced nutritional factors to meet the required needs for the health of the family hardly ever gets mentioned on the show. People of all ages find the show entertaining, but maybe quite decadent if you are poor or malnourished from lack of available healthy food or good nutritional advice.

I wonder if many people know how simple, nutritious and healthy foods taste. Suppose one's primary focus is on the richness of enhanced flavors. In that case you might as well eat Fruit Loops for breakfast, a meaty juice-dripping double cheeseburger with greasy fries for lunch, and a pepperoni, garlic bacon, and sausage pizza for dinner. Maximum flavors, lousy nutrition.

The amazing thing about our overconsumption of food in this country is that, in time, we may start to look more like some of the animals we are eating. I realize this statement is not politically correct, but being politically correct does not seem to solve the health crises we are experiencing with a large percentage of the population having preexisting health problems. With roughly one-third or more of Americans having preexisting conditions often created by their diets and the lack of sufficient exercise, we, as a country, are in poor shape. Some preexisting conditions: asthma, cancer, COPD, obesity, diabetes, sickle cell disease.

Chapter 5

RELIGION AND POLITICS: DO THEY FIT TOGETHER?

When I was young, in the 1950s, the local priests in our Catholic parish lived in a large house on a hill, drove Cadillacs, had housekeepers and cooks, were constantly invited to parishioners' parties and luncheons, and they took scheduled vacations to warm Florida during the cold months. No one ever questioned whether they were "living like examples of Christ's teachings" while the parishioners were paying their salaries to counsel them in both spiritual and nonspiritual ways.

All parochial school children were given a year's supply of tiny, coded donation envelopes into which the children were asked to place donated coins, which were then collected during every Sunday Mass they attended. With everything coded, it was just a guess that someone was keeping track of what amounts were given by each family and each child.

I doubt if Christ's Apostles, when Christ was speaking to the crowds in different locations, would be walking up to the listeners, holding a woven basket out and saying, "Hey, dude, if you don't fork over some cash, Christ might not do his gig here again." (Exaggerated emphasis for humor, but you get the point.) When I was an altar boy in grade school, for early morning Masses, there was a priest who, when you poured the wine and water into his golden chalice, would get really upset if you put more than a couple drops of water into his chalice after you had put in the wine. After Mass, he would reprimand you and advise you to hold the amount of water you poured into the wine. It felt like he was saying, "Kid, you're diluting my buzz, so only a couple of drops of water, OK?"

It was prior to 440AD that the increased roles and powers of the Popes of Christianity started. In 452, Pope Leo I negotiated with Attila the Hun to withdraw his forces from the Italian peninsula instead of attacking Rome. Pope Leo I also negotiated with Gaiseric the Vandal. In 592, Pope Gregory I negotiated with the invading Lombards. From 756 to 1870, the Papal States in Italy were run by the Popes. Around 800, Charlemagne established the Holy Roman Empire. It was not until 1059, one thousand years after Christ died that Pope Nicolas II denounced the selling of clerical posts, the marriage of the clergy, and corruption in Papal elections. Then things really started changing.

The Popes became powerful governmental rulers. They started excommunicating other political rulers to manipulate them for the Pope's own wants and needs. The Popes supported military campaigns against other peoples, religions, and nations. At times there were several men acting as Pope. In fact, at one point, there were three Popes ruling the people in different regions. Some of the Popes even had mistresses and children. Over time, the Papacy became very wealthy, exhibiting great powers with more corruption and less spiritual authority. They led Crusades against heretics and Inquisitions in France, including the one against Joan of Arc. Then there was the Spanish Inquisition in 1478, where Pope Sixtus IV, who constructed the Sistine Chapel, authorized Ferdinand and Isabella to convert Spanish Jews to Christianity. This is the same Isabella who helped Christopher Columbus sail to the Americas, which, over a short period of time, caused the deaths of tens of thousands of indigenous people and instituted slavery in the New World. On the island of Espanola, now known as Haiti and the Dominican Republic, the population of indigenous people was 100,000 when Columbus landed there in 1492. By 1514, the indigenous population was 20,000, and by 1542, there were only 200 indigenous people left.[29]

If you are interested in a real wakeup of the history of the Popes, check out the British Documentary on Amazon called: "Saints and Sinners – the History of the Popes."

The wealth of the Pope's domain is now in the hundreds of billions of dollars, yet maybe even trillions because much of what is in the Vatican is priceless. Papal conquests in the past developed a policy of ruling by authoritarianism and military might. The Pope's obedient followers waged wars, forced indoctrination, started and supported slavery, and manipulated the rulers of various countries, all done under the claim that these Popes were inspired to act these ways by Christ, the Savior.

What is the difference between what the Popes did to keep control and build wealth by plunder and death and what today's terrorists do when they also say that what they do is inspired by their God? This is the thing about large-scale organized religions when they say that God is the one inspiring them. They can justify in their minds that whatever they are doing or saying is the true path their God is telling them to follow.

You would think that with all these different types of Christian Churches and Denominations in the United States, all these believers who claim to be Christians would be behaving according to what Christ taught 2000 years ago. But this is not necessarily the case.

We need to talk about the basic principles of the Seven Deadly Sins, which are said to be fatal to spiritual progress. Ask yourself if your spiritual or political leaders are committing any of these sins.

PRIDE – The biblical definition of pride is "an inordinate self-esteem, an unreasonable feeling of superiority as to one's talents."[30]

ENVY – Biblical definition: "a feeling of disconnect and ill will because of another's advantages, possessions, etc."[31]

GLUTTONY – Biblical definition: "over-indulgence or lack of self-restraint in food, drink or wealth items, especially as status tokens."[32]

LUST – "uncontrolled or illicit sexual desire or appetite, dependence on pornography."[33]

ANGER or wrath – "Strong emotional reaction of displeasure, often leading to plans for revenge or punishment."[34]

GREED – "an overwhelming urge to have more of something, usually more than you really need. Often connected with money, a desire to acquire as much of it as possible, but it can refer to that kind of urge toward anything like food or material possessions."[35]

SLOTH – "A habitual disinclination to exertion or laziness, the word is a two-edged sword: (1) abandonment of self: we become so caught up in fear that we walk away from the things our heart truly desires and bypass opportunities. The other edge of the sword is: (2) self-absorption: once we find ourselves in that dark wilderness, we try to rationalize where we are and why. Slothfulness steals our excitement and joy in the purpose God has for us."[36]

We also need to talk about Judaism since we have mentioned what was going on with Christianity, the Seven Deadly Sins, and Christ's teachings as preached by the Apostles. It seems that none of the philosophical writings that evolved in Judaism were ever finalized or universally authorized at any formal convention or gathering of Judaism scholars or rabbis. In contrast, what developed in Christianity were the three decrees of The Apostles Creed, the Nicene or Constantinopolitan Assembly, and the Athanasian Decree.

Judaism has four main branches: Orthodox, Conservative, Reform, and Reconstructionist, with possible off-shoots. In many ways, you determine what you want to believe, depending on which of the four branches you feel is right for you. So, I am going to use the results of one event that occurred in the Old Testament that is probably accepted by all forms of Judaism.

The Ten Commandments are a group of biblical standards related to morals, ethics, and the worship of one God. They are fundamental in Abrahamic religions, appearing twice in the Hebrew Bible, in Exodus and Deuteronomy. They are the basis of Jewish Law "written with the finger of God." Exodus 31:18. Simplified, the Ten Commandments cover:

IDOLATRY – do not worship idols.
ADULTERY – be faithful to your wife or husband.

MURDER – do not commit murder or inflict serious harm on others.

TAKING – do not steal.

HONOR – obey and respect your parents.

ENVY – do not be jealous.

LIE – do not ever lie.

ONE – there is only one God to worship.

REST – rest on the Sabbath or Holy Day.

DISRESPECT – do not use God's name in vain.[37]

So, between the Ten Commandments and the Seven Deadly Sins, we have an outline of what activities God would like us to follow and how not to behave on our path through life. I would like to talk about some of The Ten Commandments in association with the loss of Common Sense in modern American culture.

IDOLATRY – There does not have to be a "golden calf," as described in the Old Testament, or a picture or statue for someone to have idolatrous practices or beliefs. Your idolatry could be with money, fame, good looks (as defined by you), a home, a car, or jewelry. Your golden calf does not have to be gold at all – it could even be yourself.

ADULTERY – Some people believe adultery involves more than husbands and wives. In Matthew 5:27-28 Christ said: "everyone who looks at a woman lustfully has already committed adultery with her in his heart." What is in your heart when you have multiple sex partners, brag about your sexual "conquests" to your friends, or hook-up with strangers in bars for lusting adventures? Are you respecting these people, treating them like you would like to be treated? Would you like your sister or mother to be treated this way? Many people in our country view having a lot of sexual encounters as insignificant and normal behavior, but in other countries, this type of behavior is considered deeply sacrilegious, immoral, and/or criminal.

MURDER – There are all types of murder and degrees of it. You can voluntarily destroy another person or yourself slowly over a long period of time by overusing and abusing food, drugs, alcohol, or doing too much of substance, even water. If you physically disable a person, you are taking away or destroying their ability to live a normal life or to take care of themselves. You can put a person in a coma where basically they have no more life awareness. There are many ways a person can intentionally cause another person to psychologically and emotionally lose their minds.

TAKING – Stealing, robbing, embezzling, plundering, diverting, abducting, and kidnapping are all activities associated with taking. Whether it is done by a little kid taking money out of his mother's wallet without her knowing about it, embezzling connected with any person or business, plundering associated with invading other countries or someone's home or giving improper stock, bond, or annuity recommendations that hurt someone but help you or your business associates. Taking could involve land, possessions, one's dignity, or civil rights.

ONE – There is only one God. When you pray for evil to happen to someone or any nation, minority, or class of people, you are not praying to or loving God. If you believe in many gods and try to establish relationships with them through witchcraft, sorcery, or Ouija Boards, you are searching for god-like entities, believing in their powers.

REST – When I was young, only a few stores were open on Sundays. Businesses wanted to have their employees rest and spend time with their families. They saw this activity as an asset to their business's well-being and company loyalty. Yes, it was considered a "family togetherness day," and where I lived, you could not buy alcohol on a Sunday. Our family went to church on Sunday, ate meals together, and connected with each other on various levels. We played cards, board games, talked to each other during meals, went for a walk together or drove outside the city to see how others lived, or to see more of Mother Nature.

RESPECT – When I was young, you hardly ever heard swearing with people using the name of God or Jesus, nor did you hear many of those sexual four-letter words. "Sh_t" was probably the most used slang word, especially if you stepped on some feces from a dog. Your parents taught you to respect others, like addressing adults using the words "Sir or Ma'am" when in conversation and not having tantrums in public. You learned that as you got older, wiser, and more mature with age, both your privileges and responsibilities increased.

There is one more area of religion that needs to be covered: the subject of televangelism. The word "televangelist" was used by TIME Magazine in 1952 to describe Roman Catholic Bishop Fulton Sheen's persona because of the mannerisms he used that were appealing on television.[38]

With the great acceptance of radio in the 1920s, missionaries found the medium favorable to their goals of reaching large numbers of people, especially where Christianity was banned. During the Great Depression of the 1930s, revivalist tent preaching became popular and produced an income for preachers. Noted radio preachers in the 1920s were S. Parkes Cadman and Aimee Semple McPherson, both of whom started out as tent preachers. Later, other popular preachers on the radio were Father Charles Coughlin, Bob Jones Sr., Ralph W. Sockman, G.E. Lawman, Charles Fuller, and Bishop Fulton J. Sheen.[39]

In 1952, Rex Humbard had a weekly service on television. By 1980, his programs reached 695 television stations in 91 languages. By 1957, Oral Roberts had 80% of the possible TV audience.[40]

The rise of Evangelical Christianity brought out newer types of Televangelists. These new preachers became very controversial, so much so that on December 7, 2009, preacher John MacArthur published a critical article on the subject called "A Colossal Fraud."

"Somebody needs to say this plainly. The faith healers and health-and-wealth preachers who dominate religious television are shameless frauds. Their message is not the true Gospel of Jesus Christ. There is nothing spiritual or miraculous about their on-stage chicanery. It is all a devious ruse designed to take advantage of desperate people. They are not Godly ministers but greedy impostors who corrupt the Word of God for money's sake. They are not real pastors who shepherd the flock of God but hirelings whose only design is to fleece the sheep. Their love of money is glaringly obvious in what they say as well as how they live. They claim to possess great spiritual power, but in reality, they are rank materialists and enemies of everything holy."[41]

The ten richest televangelists in the world are each worth $40-740 million dollars. The second ten richest $20-40 million. The third richest is $5-20 million. Today, these estimates of wealth may be higher.

If you do not know a lot about the gamesmanship of some traveling tent evangelists, watch the 1992 movie "Leap of Faith" with Steve Martin and Debra Winger. There is another type of preacher: prosperity gospel or prosperity theology televangelists, who sometimes present an image and message like what a Fortune 500 Company CEO might address to the employees of his company. Check out some of the $5-10 million dollar homes and $350,000 cars owned by these pastors. Is this what today's living in the image of Christ has become?

Although Christ taught pathways of behavior to achieve spiritual enlightenment, neither He nor His Apostles seemed to be asking for money or status for themselves, nor did they preach that monetary wealth was the goal for those who followed Christ's teachings. These followers were dedicated believers in Christ's Word, with many willing to give up their lives and die for their beliefs. How many Christians today are willing to do that? The Original Christ was the true Christian and true teacher because He practiced what He preached by example.

If politicians and corporate businesses were living their faith, whether it be Christianity or Judaism, they would not be having affairs outside of their marriage, taking bribes, or accepting illegal campaign contributions. They would be primarily looking out for the poorer, weaker, and less educated of our population rather than listening to and catering to the "fat cats" who are at the top of the political and economic echelons of our American society.

What behaviors did Christ advocate for people to become better Christians? The Gospel of Matthew 5:3-10 says: "Blessed are the poor in spirit for theirs is the kingdom of heaven. Blessed are those who mourn, for they will be comforted. Blessed are the meek, for they will inherit the earth. Blessed are those who hunger and thirst for righteousness, for they will be satisfied. Blessed are the merciful, for they will be shown mercy. Blessed are the pure of heart, for they will see God. Blessed are the peacemakers, for they will be called children of God. Blessed are those who are persecuted because of righteousness', for theirs is the kingdom of heaven."

POLITICIANS VERSUS TRUTH TELLERS

Most politicians are not truth-tellers. Though I believe that many politicians are liars, I am going to phrase it as "not truth-tellers." If I were to say that some politicians are truth-tellers, then most non-truth-tellers would claim to be truth-tellers. For two centuries in America, not telling the truth has become almost a mandatory trait for political success. It is part of the game that politicians in office play to get elected and stay in office for many years. If all politicians were truth seekers and speakers, there would be fewer criminal behaviors. Our citizens would be a lot healthier, better educated, and more honest and caring toward their fellow countrymen. There would be greater harmony in the way people treat each other, no matter what color or race they might be. If there were more "Honest Abe" politicians who worked for the welfare of everyone, America would be a much different country than it is now.

Most people in the United States want to view their leaders as positive examples of good leadership and character, and, as such, it makes citizens want to follow the guidelines of those who are ruling the country. A leader may say he is doing what is best for the citizens, but his policies may not reflect that. Americans are learning that you cannot believe in and follow politicians who are not leaders for all the people.

When any person gets elected or reelected to the Presidency, he is generally a reflection of the populace or the desire of the populace to put someone in office who will change how the government functions. The Electoral College is not a reflection of the total voting populace. It is a method of how political elections can be manipulated to achieve victory in the Electoral College, especially when a candidate may not win the popular vote. The methods used for districting and redistricting a state for the purpose of selecting Electoral College voters are a function of each state's choice. The methods vary not only from state to state, but they also vary within states. There are 37 states where the state legislature has the prime responsibility for redistricting. Independent commissions determine district boundaries in six states, and political commissions determine boundaries in 7 states. In some states, the Governor has the power to veto how the district boundaries are set; in other states, he can't.

There is also the practice of gerrymandering, which is an activity where one state's majority political party can redraw the district boundaries in their favor. Gerrymandering is often used to help or hurt certain groups or classes. A state political party may either favor or dismiss groups connected to ethnic, monetary, racial, linguistic, or religious backgrounds. Incumbents can also be favored through gerrymandering. If you want to see the difference between what a politically drawn district looks like now in contrast to what they would look like fairly drawn if based on where the population is located, go to this website reference.[42]

States also make independent determinations of who is eligible to vote, where the actual voting locations are established, and even the process by which candidates can or cannot get on the ballot. These factors can all be used as political power plays constructed by the top politicians in either small or large voting districts. Politicians often create certain voting requirements that are not for the benefit of the populace but for their personal party's benefit. These political decisions often produce more favorable opportunities for one political party to dominate whatever legislative membership they choose.

There are two types of lying that politicians can use in their exchanges with the public. First, there are lies of commission – a politician straight out says something that is not true. The second type of lie is by omission, whereby the politician knows about something that might affect the public or himself in a negative way, but he withholds the information when questioned about it. He may withhold the truth because it might get him in legal, moral, or political trouble or negatively affect how voters respect him; therefore, he omits it when questioned. A politician's omissions may also occur because of "deals" he has made with other politicians, friends, corporations, or sexual contacts.

The way that our political election system is currently set up, with its exorbitant costs, extremely long campaign periods, and the dilemma that you can win the popular vote by millions of votes through democratic voting procedures but lose the election, really questions the validity of one's personal vote. The more politicians lie and continue those lies to specific groups in specific states, the more they increase their chances of winning the Electoral College.

Did you know that in other countries, the political campaign season is limited to three to six months before the election date, and prior campaigning is not allowed before that time? The longer the campaign period, the easier it is for politicians to manipulate the voting public, the more it costs a candidate to participate in an election, and the harder it is to understand the many altered positions a candidate offers over time.

Think about the following quotes which reflect aspects of why many politicians run for office:

"Power is the great aphrodisiac."[43]

-Henry Kissinger

"The Power to define the situation is the ultimate power."[44]

-J. Rubin

"The power to do good is also the power to do harm; those who control the power today may not tomorrow; and more important, what one man regards as good, another may regard as harm."[45]

-Milton Friedman

So, what about corporate fibs to the public? Let us use pharmaceutical companies as an example. There have been many products and drugs that have been produced by pharmaceutical companies over the years that have been withdrawn from the marketplace because they have done physical harm. A simple Google search found 73 drugs banned in the United States and removed from the marketplace since 1963.

The United States Library of Medicine, part of the National Institute of Health, has a report saying that between 1950 and 2013, 462 medical products were withdrawn after they had been marketed in the United States. I then looked at some of the popular drugs that were sold to consumers for long periods of time before they were "Taken Off the Market," how they were used, and who made and marketed them.

Darvon, Darvocet – opioid for pain relief, on the market for 55 years, 1955-2010 Hoffman-LaRoche

DES – synthetic estrogen, on the market for 31 years, 1949-1971. Grant Chemical Co.

PTZ and Metrazol – therapy for schizophrenia, on the market for 48 years, 1932-1982

Quaalude – sedative/hypnotic, on the market for 23 years, 1962-1985, William H Rorer Inc and Lemmon Co.

"Each year, more than 2 million serious adverse drug reactions occur in the United States, causing an estimated 100,000 deaths. Many safety problems emerge only after drugs have received Food and Drug Administration (FDA) approval…The FDA approves new drugs significantly faster than the regulatory bodies of Europe, Canada, and Japan. Unlike the United States, most European Union countries require that new drugs undergo a secondary review process comparing their efficacy to the existing standard of care before health insurance plans will pay for them. Furthermore, the European Union, Canada, and Japan prohibit direct-to-consumer advertising, which is known to increase prescribing of the advertised drug…Hence, many Americans may be exposed to drugs that pose a risk to their health before their dangers are adequately appreciated."[46]

Every day, especially on television, we are constantly flooded with drug advertising. Drug companies love to put their ads on the national evening news because a large audience of viewers can produce bigger profits. "If you have any of the symptoms we have mentioned during this commercial, then go ask your doctor to prescribe the drug just advertised. It may solve your problem." Of course, some of the side effects may compound your health problems or even kill you, but maybe you will be lucky. Watch these ads and see how they can distract and deceive viewers at the same time. They distract you by showing you a group of family and friends having a great smiley time with children, grandparents, or friends of all ages, frolicking around, all smiles and joyfulness, no one sick or crippled, generally no one obese, with beautiful skin and hair, without a negative care in the world, just enjoying a bountiful life.

While you are visualizing that, they may be verbally running through complications or negative drug interactions. "You may break out in hives, rashes, become light-headed, get constipated, have diarrhea, feel pains in your arms or legs, lose your ability to speak, develop heart problems, lose consciousness, or die. Do not take this drug if you are allergic to any of the ingredients. (How do you know if you have never used the drug?) Seek medical help in an emergency room if needed, but thanks for buying it and making our shareholders wealthier. Have a nice day."

When I moved about ten years ago, I changed doctors because of a change in location. When I went in for my first visit, which was only for a Medicare Wellness checkup, I had to fill out the paperwork that they handed me. I answered all the questions and returned the paperwork to the nurse. A little while later, the doctor came in, shook my hand, then started to read my paperwork. After a while, he stopped and said, "You forgot to fill out the prescription drugs you are taking." I said, "I don't take any prescription drugs or NSAIDS, Tylenol, or Opioids." Then he said something that really got to me. "You are the very first patient over 65 I have ever treated in my practice who takes no prescription drugs." That was when I knew that this great country of ours was in real trouble.

I did a year of Pharmacy School in college, and then one day, the head of the Department came into one of the pharmacy classes and gave us a lecture about the importance of the deals that are worked out between Pharmacists and distributors of Pharmaceutical Drugs. That was it for me. Time to change my future profession and life direction.

Do you know how many legal drug prescriptions were filled in the United States in 2021? The answer is around 4.7 billion. This works out to about 13 prescriptions per American, but only about 65% of Americans use prescriptions. The numbers in 2022 and 2023 were even larger. What does that say about the health of our country?

It is getting hard these days to believe in many politicians or corporate leaders. Fibs are adding up to the thousands. Our leaders are starting to sound and act more aristocratic and self-centered. Whatever happened to them working for the "welfare and happiness of all the people?"

The bigger question is: Why do so many of our citizens believe all the lies, ill-spoken exaggerations, derogatory put-downs of women, bad health recommendations, and abusive language that is used against minorities and other countries by our politicians? Here is a possible answer.

Today, American society is so overwhelmed with choices of what to buy, what to do, where to go, how to live, and who's social and/or moral philosophies a citizen should follow that we now live in a state that psychologists call "the paradox of choice." When we allow too many choices into our decision-making rationale, our self-created confusion opens us up to accepting mistaken philosophies and political ideologies from leaders who tell us what to do, say, or think for their own benefit.

We abandon much of our unique personal identity and the ability for introspection and self-guidance in favor of following the words of a biased and elitist political or cult leader or the actions of a crowd. This behavioral pattern is historically repeated whenever citizens become addicted to leaders who claim they are the only people with the correct philosophies and solutions for everyone in their country.

Below is a small list of major leaders in the 20th Century whose citizens believed in, endorsed, let themselves be seduced by, or who followed their leaders "to hell" until their country's leadership was overthrown. Yet there are many cases where those who did the overthrowing became just as bad or corrupt as the previous rulers. This occurred because the overall citizenry in many countries still believed that resignation to political propaganda was easier to accept and follow than studying and learning from history's past manipulations of naïve or uninformed citizens.

What do Americans have to fear from learning both American and world history? Wouldn't it be beneficial for your own welfare to learn from all the mistakes other citizens in our society made that caused their social and economic lives to deteriorate?

Here is a short list of leaders' names and the fundamental philosophical approach they used to persuade their citizens to follow them instead of following their own personal beliefs or the beliefs of someone else.

Hitler-	Make Germany Great Again
Stalin –	Make Russia Great Again
Mussolini –	Make Italy Great Again
Kim Il-Sung -	Make North Korea Great Again
Mao Zedong -	Make China Great Again

Where have we heard this before?

Listen to what today's politicians of either party in the United States are saying to the citizenry. Both parties are playing the same game by saying: vote for us because we know what is best for you.

Why are there only two major political parties in the U.S.? The two parties have an unwritten contract for each party to maintain power and control at different periods of time when their party becomes a majority. This approach allows them to exclude any third party from having any type of political leadership position. The current two-party system thus creates a political monopoly in which they periodically trade off leadership with each other over time, thereby granting each party the ability to create and maintain dominance of power for only themselves without great interference from the other political party. If there was a third major political party, all three parties would be virtually mandated to cooperate and compromise with each other to achieve positive regulations and governing laws for the betterment of ALL Americans, both rich and poor.

Years ago, there was greater compromise between the Democrats and Republicans because they understood that they were elected to serve the entire nation, not just themselves, their rich friends, or their "tribes." Back then, politicians and corporate leaders possessed greater morals and ethics in their political undertakings, which historically are the backbone of a positive, healthy, and prosperous nation. Today, the internet gives you thousands of reasons or options to choose otherwise, and tribalism reinforces those choices by favoring "us versus them" outcomes.

A HISTORICAL REMEMBERANCE RELATIVE TO TODAY

Adolph Hitler's book "Mein Kampf" (My Struggle) was written in 1925 while he was in prison after he was convicted of high treason for trying to overthrow the German Republic in 1923. From 1925 to 1945, this book sold 12 million copies and was printed in at least 12 languages.

In his book, Hitler talks about "The Big Lie," which seems to have been conceptionally relevant in American politics for over four years. He wrote that the great masses "will more easily fall victims to a great lie than to a small one since they themselves perhaps also lie sometimes in little things but would certainly still be too much ashamed of too great lies. Thus, such an untruth will not at all enter their heads, and therefore, they will be unable to believe in the possibility of the enormous impudence of the most infamous distortion in others."

Political propaganda becomes unjustifiable when one party claims that the so-called big lie is the big truth, even when all legal court actions deny their claims. Hitler showed us how his big lies were readily accepted by the German population, who were willing to die in war for the claims of their leader. After all, this German leader was going to create a stronger economy, lower inflation, increase worker wages, ban freedom-seeking, different skin-colored, aliens from entering the country, and "Make Germany Great Again."

We all know how this scenario ended. The Big Lie in Germany survived from 1925 to 1945. Will Americans become so mesmerized by a single leader of any political party that they follow a similar path?

Chapter 6

CAPITALISM, POLITICIANS, AND CORPORATIONS

Income inequality is the result of how and why capitalism works best for the richest among us. If you want to change income inequality, you may have to make changes in how capitalism works. Our current American economics is based on a "capitalism for me" platform. The following, from Englishman David Harvey's book "Seventeen Contradictions and the End of Capitalism," analyzes how capital, the wealth of investors and entrepreneurs, is "socially and historically constructed as a class in dominance over labour. The distribution of income and of wealth between capital and labour has to be lopsided if capital is to be reproduced…Any drive to maximize profits means driving down wage rates or increasing labour productivity…A disproportionate amount of the surplus must always flow to capital at the expense of labour…inequality is foundational for investors' prosperity…A sufficient share of the total output of social value must flow to the capitalist class to incentivize the capitalists by showering them with conditions of consumption worthy of some leisure class."[47]

During the last Recession, Capital either "warehoused its cash or used its surplus incomes for speculative gains on the stock market, in property, in asset purchases (resources and land in particular), or in playing a casino game with new and unstable financial instruments."[48]

"Meanwhile, the increasing concentration and centralization of income and wealth within a capitalist class permitted it to exercise disproportionate influences and control over the media (public opinion) and capitalist state apparatus (government). Capital procured privileged access to protection by a state which claims a monopoly over the legitimate use of violence and a monopoly over the means of money creation. It uses these privileges to protect its interests and perpetuate its power. This is what the drift towards the formation of a global plutocracy and the incredible increases in the disparity of wealth and income in most countries around the world signals."[49]

While you may think that some of this is far-fetched, just remember one thing: during and after the last recession, for all the lost homes, lost jobs, lost incomes, losses of people's health, and the resulting numbers of people who would wind up living in tents or in their cars after being kicked out of their homes, did any of the bank executives and mortgage executives who created and pushed complex, guaranteed to lose money investments, CDOs, underfunded and inappropriate mortgage contracts, or placing you in spurious bank accounts that you did not authorize – did any of these manipulators go to jail for the millions of citizens that they deceived or ripped-off? NO. Did any of the government leaders who were supposed to regulate the banks, mortgage lending companies, or brokerage companies to protect the American public from dishonesty get punished with jail time or heavily fined? NO. Did the President of the United States, at the time all this was going on, call out, verbally or on paper, the regulators, bankers, or brokerage companies for their indiscretions and failings? NO. The opposite happened.

When the administration changed, many of these same regulators and administrators left their government jobs with big pensions and went to work for the same banks and brokerages that they were originally supposed to regulate. The bank and brokerage company executives received big bonuses. Over time these rich buyers, who had bought the public's super-discounted, now lost homes, later sold or rented them for huge profits.

These are the types of things that "Capitalism for Me" can do to a society. American citizens once believed that the United States government and the business community were responsibly looking out for Mr. and Mrs. Average Citizen. But as income inequality keeps getting bigger between the haves and have-nots, many people are realizing that American capitalism is not working very well for them. A survey done in March of 2023 found that 58% of Americans are living paycheck to paycheck. Another survey in July 2023 found 78% earning less than $50,000 and 65% earning between $50,000 and $100,000 living paycheck to paycheck.

How about "happiness"? When Thomas Jefferson wrote the Declaration of Independence, what were the most radical ideas advocated by a colony wanting to become a new nation? "All men are created equal, that they are endowed by their Creator with certain inalienable Rights, that among these are Life, Liberty, and the pursuit of Happiness."

According to the World Happiness Report, released by the Sustainable Development Solutions Network of the United Nations (3-20-2023), countries are ranked in six key variables: income, freedom, trust, healthy life expectations, social support, and generosity. They also use emotional measures of well-being. The top ten happiest countries 2022 and 2023:

1 Finland (2022)	1 Finland (2023)
2 Denmark	2 Denmark
3 Iceland	3 Iceland
4 Switzerland	4 Israel
5 Netherlands	5 Netherlands
6 Luxembourg	6 Sweden
7 Sweden	7 Norway
8 Norway	8 Switzerland
9 Israel	9 Luxembourg
10 New Zealand	10 New Zealand

In Finland, they pay high taxes for a social safety net, trust their government, live in freedom, and are generous with each other. Co-author John Helliwell said: "That's the place people want to live. No matter whether we look at the state of democracy and political rights, lack of corruption, trust between citizens, felt safety, social cohesion, gender equality, equal distribution of incomes, Human Development Index, or many other global comparisons, one tends to find the Nordic countries in the global top spots."[50]

In the 2023 Report, the United States ranked 15th, but it ranked low in social support, low in healthy life expectancy, low in freedom and ranked poorly in corruption. There were no superpowers ranked in the top 10; the United Kingdom was 19th, Germany was 16th, Japan was 55th, Russia was 74th, and China was 82nd. In the 2024 report America dropped to 23rd.

For "Capitalism for Me" to work well, you need a lot of poor and lower middle-class people. The members of our Upper Classes in America, to justify their position in society, have falsely created the fantasy statement that: "You too can be rich like us, you just have to work hard." The people at the top do not mention things like huge inheritances for them and their children, the easy ability to pay for their children to attend the best universities in the country, their political, social, and corporate connections that provide them with "favors," insider information, and large donations to political campaigns to get the "you scratch my back, and I'll scratch yours" benefits.

Was "Capitalism for Me," the way it is practiced today, always this way in the United States? I do know that after World War II, until around 1965-75, Americans built a lot of quality merchandise. During those decades, companies in America bragged in their advertisements that they wanted to produce what was best for both the consumer and the country. Middle-class Americans prospered with overall higher wages.

Most moms could stay home and focus on raising their children in wholesome, moral, and ethical ways. Dad's paycheck could provide for the family, schooling for most of the children, and maybe even a family vacation. The TV shows that the family watched, such as "Father Knows Best," "Leave It to Beaver, and "Ozzie and Harriet," showed examples of family unity and how to handle the variety of life problems that family members encountered. Shows like "Rawhide" and "Wagon Train" taught children about historical periods in American History, showing how

Americans struggled moving out west, with every show describing either how to overcome adversity or how to use moral and ethical ways to solve problems and controversies. "Wagon Train" was so popular that when Gene Roddenberry promoted the idea of a TV series called "Star Trek," he called it "Wagon Train to the Stars." (Wagon Train can still be seen on the FETV Channel, the INSP channel, the GFAM channel, and Starz Westerns.)

In the 1950s, cars, furniture, and many homes were quality-built by experienced, lifelong craftsmen who took great pride in their work. Those 1950s homes are still sturdy today compared to later-built tract homes that were built fast and cheaply. Objects, whether they were toys, cars, or appliances, were built to last.

Mothers and fathers often helped answer their children's questions about experiences the children were having with others in school or encounters the children were having in their social lives. Family dinners played an important role in raising children. Family members talked to each other and actually paid attention to what each person was saying.

In a lot of ways, life was pretty "hunky-dory," except if you were African American, a Spanish-speaking American, or other heavily discriminated against races or nationalities. In some areas of the country, especially in the Southern parts, the rage against minorities was mostly practiced by white Democrats, a carryover from the Civil War and prewar slavery times. There have been two different Americas in our country for a long time.

Even our dedicated nonwhite soldiers who bravely fought during World War II and Korea faced many injustices after they came back from fighting for our freedoms. It was a sad event, and many innocent people were abused and unjustifiably killed by racial segregationists and white radicals. All these years later, there are still injustices against blacks and minorities suffering all over the country.

In general, during the 1950s and 1960s, manufacturing companies bragged about their products. They were quality built, made in America by some of your own parents, grandparents, and great-grandparents. People around the world wanted American products. This was a time when company CEOs were making reasonable salaries in relation to their average workers, unlike today's $20-200 million dollar salaries.

One of the best movies to watch about what typical white-collar business owners were like in the 40s and 50s is "Executive Suite," which came out in 1954. The movie had no "super action scenes," and there was no background music. It was nominated for four Academy Awards. It dealt with the basic human gut instincts of "bigger is better" versus quality control and fairness to employees and customers. If you lived in the 1950s, you lived during a period when many aspects of "Capitalism for Us" were happening. Newer versions of this type of capitalism may still be found among niche groups of smaller businesses here in this country, but you will find them more prevalent in the Nordic countries of Denmark, Sweden, Norway, and Finland. Many die-hard right-wingers think that these countries are Socialist, but that extremist view is not true.

"The Nordic countries practice mostly free economics paired with high taxes exchanged for generous government entitlement programs…These productive economies, generating good income for their workers, allowed the governments to raise the tax revenue needed to pay for the social benefits…None of these countries have minimum wage laws. Unions are reasonably powerful in many industries and negotiate contracts…The Nordic countries offer government-paid healthcare, in some cases tuition-free university education and rather generous social safety nets…Perhaps a better name for what the Nordic countries practice would be compassionate socialism." (From the article: "Sorry Bernie Bros but Nordic Countries Are Not Socialist.")[51]

There are many "socialistic type activities and agencies" that occur in the United States: Social Security, farm price supports and energy subsidies, Medicare, Medicaid, government grants, bank deposit insurance, tax loopholes for some but banned for others, minimum wage standards, municipality sponsored public housing projects, even public schools. These are democratic socialist activities widely accepted by Americans.

If you would like to know more about governmental policies around the world that work to create benefits to help citizens, check out the movie: "Where to Invade Next," by Michael Moore. I realize that there are people in America who do not like this person, but this movie is more of a travelogue as he travels to nine different countries to observe social benefits that are automatically given to citizens. A lot of these benefits for individuals and families are not available in the United States, the richest country in the world.

CAPITALISM

Conservatives often consider Adam Smith the father, creator, and patron saint of American Capitalism. Smith lived from 1723 to 1790 and was a Scottish economist, philosopher, author, and a key figure in the Era of Scottish Enlightenment. He has often been called the "Father of Economics" and the "Father of Capitalism."

In 1751, Smith was appointed professor of Logic at Glasgow University. In 1752, he became the Chair of Moral Philosophy. His book, "An Inquiry into the Nature and Causes of the Wealth of Nations," came out in 1776 and became extremely popular and influential because his philosophy of economics established an "autonomous systematic discipline" of how to deal with economic problems. He was a big advocate of free trade and allowing businessmen to seek, find, and do what was best for their business and profits: "a laissez-faire capitalism."

Smith called this a system of perfect liberty, using the desire for self-betterment guided by the faculties of reason to achieve a stable human nature. He concluded this system was the best for achieving business success. He advocated the art of using an institutional mechanism to settle any troublesome activities intrinsic in a blind acquiescence to one's devotions. This philosophical approach is what has justified the fundamentals, practices, and dominance of what America's "Capitalism for Me" is all about.

With Capitalism for Me, when a large corporation announces the layoff of 1000 or more workers, the company's stock price goes up. The executives and stockholders of the company are achieving higher company valuations and praise from their big investors because of the changes the company has made. Meanwhile, what happens to all the people who no longer have a job with the company? This same asset growth occurs when a company shuts down a plant or factory and moves to Mexico, China, or Vietnam. The company shareholders see increased valuation in their stock prices because the wealthy investment community feels that by reducing expenses with the lower salaries of the new, outside the United States factory workers, companies will achieve greater profits, which translates to higher stock prices and dividends.

What many conservatives, investors, and company CEOs do not mention about Adam Smith are the other aspects of economic business growth that Smith included in his two books: "The Wealth of Nations" and "The Theory of Moral Sentiments." Let's mention a few of the other beliefs and philosophies of Adam Smith.

In "Wealth of Nations," he writes: "Wherever there is great property (prosperity), there is great inequality. For one very rich man, there must be at least five hundred poor, and the affluence of the few supposed the indigence of the many."

In "The Theory of Moral Sentiments," he says: "This disposition to admire, and almost to worship, the rich and powerful, and to despise, or, at least, to neglect persons of poor and mean condition, though necessary both to establish and to maintain the distinction of ranks and the order of society, is, at the same time, the great and most universal cause of the corruption of our moral sentiments."

Also, in the "Wealth of Nations," he wrote: "A man must always live by his work, and his wages must at least be sufficient to maintain him. They must, even upon most occasions be somewhat more: otherwise, it would be impossible for him to bring up a family, and the race of such workmen could not last beyond the first generation."

"With the greater part of rich people, the chief enjoyment of riches consists in the parade of riches, which, in their eye, is never so complete as when they appear to possess those decisive marks of opulence which nobody can possess but themselves. In their eyes, the merit of an object, which is in any degree either useful or beautiful, is greatly enhanced by its scarcity or by the great labour which it requires to collect any considerable quantity of it, a labour which nobody can afford to pay but themselves." ("Wealth of Nations")

"Civil government, so far as it is instituted for the security of property, is in reality instituted for the defense of the rich against the poor." ("An Inquiry into the Nature and Causes of the Wealth of Nations")

How about the perceptions and philosophies of someone more modern, like Pope Francis? "The worship of the ancient golden calf has returned in a new and ruthless guise in the idolatry of money and the dictatorship of an impersonal economy lacking true human purpose…While the earnings of a minority are growing exponentially, so too is the gap separating the majority from the prosperity enjoyed by those happy few."[52]

The Pope also said this: "A new tyranny is thus born. Invisible and often virtual, which unilaterally and relentlessly imposes its own laws and rules…Has a thirst for power and possessions that knows no limit…Tends to devour everything that stands in the way of increased profits…Whatever is fragile, like the environment, is defenseless before the interests of a deified market."[53]

I wrote the following section about 20 years ago. Few people were interested then; maybe more might find it relevant today.

Many Christians do not follow Christ's teachings or New or Old Testament moral or ethical philosophies when it comes to investing their money. There are several aspects of what investments and personal monetary successes can mean to a Christian.

FINANCIAL SUCCESS – Do you realize that when you invest your money in financial instruments like the Dow Jones Industrials, the S&P 500, and the Nasdaq 100 Indices or ETFs, you may be investing in companies that might be heavy polluters of the environment, could be manufacturers of tobacco products or other products that cause cancer, sell or profit from pornography, or produce legal addictive drugs or effects that cause behavioral addictions or medical problems for the populace? A major drug problem in the United States is the abuse of legal drugs. Suppose you invest your money with these companies or the bonds of the companies. In that case, you are investing to make financial gains from the increased valuations, profit-generating dividends, or higher bond prices. The same goes for stock or bond indices or mutual funds. While you may achieve monetary gains, it may be at the expense of your fellow citizens, who may suffer from medical illnesses, addictions, or possible deaths from the exposure or abuse of company products. Would Christ have advocated investing in these companies to achieve positive monetary gains for yourself while those companies' products harm others?

PERSONAL HEALTH SUCCESS – In his teachings, do you think Christ applauded the goodness of being obese, unhealthy, or taking excessive drugs? "My children, become more gluttonous, drink more alcohol, use more tobacco products, eat more Big Macs and junk food, stop exercising, pop more legal painkillers and antidepressants, spend more hours on the Internet in addictive searches dwelling on false political and social propaganda, and it will be easier for you to enter the Kingdom of Heaven." Yet the very companies that produce the products connected to the above behaviors are the ones that financial advisors tell you to own. Yes, you will achieve financial success. Still, I do not see where investing in companies that help manifest negative behavioral addictions is among Christ's teachings for attaining spiritual growth and harmony.

EMOTIONAL PEACE OF MIND SUCCESS – Why do so many people follow the negative emotions and habits presented in today's daytime and nighttime TV or Internet programs? What about repeatedly playing violent videos and computer games or getting sexually addicted to pornography? Research has shown that these constant viewing behaviors negatively affect social mores. Christ taught the benefits of leading a calmer, more introspective life, not one that seeks out confrontational exchanges and bolstered biases. Where do Christ's teachings say you can attain peace of mind and contentment by constantly viewing violence, striving to materialistically keep up with your neighbors, or depending on unknown "like us" digital friends on screens for comfort or peace of mind?

You might think a little more about how you should be investing your money, spending your time, and using your energy. If you are claiming to be a Christian, Catholic, or Protestant, are you living the values, morals, and ethics advocated by Christ's teachings, or do you just want to make money to line your pockets and fill your bank accounts, not caring how companies make their profits? At this point, you might be reflecting on this justification: "Well, I am just investing little bits of money in these companies." When you retire, will you still have only little bits of individual company stocks in your accounts? Not really. You could have invested thousands of dollars in these companies. You and millions of similar people are investing these "little bits of money," which, over time, creates billions and trillions in asset wealth and profits for not only the investors but also the companies. What you do with your money is your choice. You may claim to be a Christian, but if you are not following the fundamentals of Christ's teachings, how can you say you are a Christian believer?

Here is an example of what I am talking about. I ran into a gentleman I had not seen in about thirty years. During our conversation, he informed me that he was a conscientious citizen, a Christian, and environmental activist who recycled, ate organic foods, and his whole family was vegetarians who drove electric cars. I was surprised to find out that his investments were mainly in S&P 500 mutual funds. So, I asked him if he thought it was fair that S&P component companies like Salesforce, Honeywell, Chevron, and IBM, among many other companies, paid no Federal Income Tax during 2019 when he had probably paid at least 20-30% on his personal Federal income tax filing.

He said he reasoned that he had to invest in these companies because they financially benefited his family, which was more important. I asked him if these investments were also good for his grandchildren and a healthy environment. He responded: "I am just doing what my financial advisor is telling me to do." Then he walked away. Maybe claiming you are a Christian, a vegetarian, and an environmentalist isn't as ethically important as having a lot of money.

STOCK AND BOND MARKET

Stock markets, bond markets, mutual funds, options markets, and commodity futures markets are designed, maintained, and controlled by savvy, wealthy, and technical people who operate and control the investment roulette wheels. Their main objective is to make money for themselves, their companies, and their richest investors. Then there are the TV financial programs, especially CNBC, Fox Business, and Bloomberg. These programs are mainly vehicles for short-term stock and bond market traders who want profits quickly, in a few days, months, or a few years. Most average investment owners are long-term stockholders and bondholders. Buy-and-hold investments are too boring for these shows.

In general, smaller, long-term investors with IRAs, 401Ks, or some other non-governmental work/savings vehicles are told to buy and hold their investments, slowly liquidating small percentages after they retire 5 to 50 or more years from now.

Of course, this procedure is not necessarily what the financial world's wealthy investors and traders do. Have you ever watched one of the business channels to see what happens when there is big news, whether it might indicate panic or prosperity, that might influence the wealthy to think more about their money than normal? (That last statement may be hard to believe.) Asset prices fluctuate wildly, moving up or down in fast multi-million-dollar increments. A market like the Dow Jones Industrial Average can move one or two hundred or even a thousand points up or down faster than you can say the word: Dow. Why is this occurring? Are people acting so skittish that they want to change their minds minute by minute, or second by second, to try and figure out if the market is going to make big jumps up or down in the next couple of seconds or minutes? The fact is that most of the activity or volume of trading that takes place in financial markets is controlled by machines – Artificial Intelligence computers that do most of the buying and selling almost automatically in microseconds.

Years ago, when you watched the financial channels, they showed the stock ticker tape on the bottom of your TV screen. It had the stock name abbreviation, the price change, and the number of shares sold in that trade. When the big boys were trading, you could see single trades of 10,000 shares or more. Today, these stock quantities are generally not provided. Now, you mostly see the stock and price changes. Though you might not see the shares exchanged in a single trade, brokerage houses and people who spend big bucks can receive all the information available. Nowadays, you can have multiple huge monitors at your desk showing what is happening in markets around the world. Instantly available information can often be one of the best keys to success. The optimal goal is to own Artificial Intelligence computers programmed by experts in certain critical ways that can basically think and react on their own, generating trades and profits in less time than a tenth of a second.

These AI machines can create their own "volatility." Traders can experience huge money-making opportunities in the stock market when volatility occurs. A lot of big money gains can also occur when stocks are going down rapidly because you are selling to a lot of small-funded people who are mostly just buying. Unlike the little players, who are told to buy stocks until they retire and then sell them to make their profits, the big guys want the profits now: in the next couple of seconds, in ten minutes, by tomorrow, or before the end of the three-month quarter.

Here is the problem. Unless you have a lot of money, and I mean a lot, you will generally not be given the opportunity to do what the big boys can do. First, you need a brokerage account funded with a lot of cash. Secondly, you need to hire the right kinds of people. Thirdly, you might have to risk losing hundreds of thousands of dollars or more to make a million dollars in profits on your trades. These factors automatically limit the number of people who can play the game.

There are many ways to make money in financial markets besides buying and selling stocks. There is the Options Market. With options, you can bet whether a stock, an index (Dow Jones, S&P 500, Nasdaq 100), or a commodity will go up or down over a length of time. You can even bet that an investment product will not go either up or down in value. Here are some of the names of betting styles you can use in the Options Market, but trying to explain how these option trades work is very complex.

1. Buy a naked call.
2. Do a converted call.
3. Do a married put.

4. Do a Bull call spread.
5. Do a Bear put spread.
6. Do a protective collar.
7. Do a long straddle.
8. Do a long strangle.
9. Do a long call.
10. Do a butterfly spread.
11. Do an Iron Condor.
12. Do an Iron Butterfly.

Are you now confused? Rich people in brokerage companies have invented many complex techniques for making money in the markets. There are also Commodity Futures Markets based on commodities and stock indexes, for example, where you only need to put up a small percentage of the value of an index or a commodity to buy or sell it. (More on this later in the book.)

BONDS   The biggest financial market in the United States is the Bond Market. "What? You are wrong," people say, "No way, it's the stock market! Stock market activity and daily results are emphasized and reported to us every day in newspapers, TV programs, and every moment on the TV business channels." Yes, these business TV channels talk to the public using stock advisors, mutual fund managers, and stock commentators. They talk all day long about stocks in the Dow Jones, the S&P 500, and the Nasdaq exchanges. Yes, the stock markets are the flashy, headline-getting, newsy markets that draw the attention of both investors and non-investors. Before understanding bonds, you need to know about the inequality of stock ownership and what average citizens own. In 2021, only about 56% of American adults owned stocks, ETFs, or mutual funds. (In 2022, it was about 58%.) From 2001-2008 the average was 62%. According to the Federal Reserve Bank, in 2021, the top 10% of the wealthiest Americans owned 89% of all stocks in the United States. The bottom 90% of Americans owned about 11% of the stocks.

The Federal Reserve has an interesting historical chart on the wealth of Americans: How much wealth is owned by whom? This chart starts with 1989 Q3 (Q3 stands for the third quarter of the fiscal calendar year),

Top wealthiest	1% in 1989 owned	$4.88	trillion.
Bottom	50% in 1989 owned	$0.76	trillion.
Top wealthiest	1% in 2009 owned	$16.33	trillion.
Bottom	50% in 2009 owned	$0.53	trillion.
Top wealthiest	1% in 2019 owned	$34.85	trillion.
Bottom	50% in 2019 owned	$1.53	trillion.[54]

In the 30 years from Q3 1989 to Q3 2019, the wealth of the top 1% increased by 714%, and the wealth of the bottom 50% increased by 201%. In every decade in those 30 years, income inequality massively increased. For Q3 2022, the top 1% owned $41.38 trillion, and the bottom 50% owned $4.52 trillion.

How people participate in the bond market is one of the factors that contribute to increasing wealth inequality. Most average investors buy bonds for stable income.

Most financial advisors tell you to treat your bonds like your stocks. Ladder your bonds, hold them to maturity, and buy another one to continue your bond ladder of Treasuries or corporate bonds. Laddering bonds means that you buy bonds to replace bonds that are maturing. For example, you could buy bonds that mature in 1, 5, or 10 years. Then, whenever a bond matures you buy another to replace it maturing in 5 or 10 years. By holding the bond to maturity, you get back all you invested. Or you could buy a bond fund that does not have a set yield, and the worth of the bond might fluctuate up or down. With bond funds, you can gain or lose money depending on when you need the money and when you are withdrawing money from the fund.

Then there are the rich bond investors who, with the help of paid brokers and AI computers, can get you into a sophisticated program of Trading Bonds. In the last 30 years, trading bonds have allowed many rich people to receive 5-30% yields every year. In a short-term example, if you had bought a 10-year Treasury at the beginning of 2020, you would have gotten a yield of 2.30%. If you sold that same Treasury on 7-21-2020, which was then yielding 0.605%, you would have made a lot of money.

You may be wondering how you could make money when you bought a Treasury at 2.30% and sold it at 0.605%. It's because bonds operate in the opposite way of stocks. As bond yields go down, the price of the bond goes up, and the more the yields go down, the greater the monetary return a person gets because their low-yield bonds are now priced so much higher. Rich investors were heavily buying bonds for decades as the yield kept dropping for U.S. Treasures, then selling them for huge profits. When bond yields greatly increased, that changed the picture.

But then, with a big jump in inflation, bond prices (costs) decreased, and yields went higher because the Federal Reserve had to increase their Federal Funds Rates to stop or slow down rising inflation. At least, that is their hope. The huge increase in Fed Fund rates caused mortgages and credit card rates to vastly increase from 12-20 months ago. The rates as of 10/2023 doubled. But then, with dreams of no more rate increases from the Fed, speculators piled into buying bonds, looking for higher prices later in 2024-25 so they might cash in their bonds for financial gains.

The total United States Bond Market is much larger than the United States stock markets. You may be asking yourself: "Well, if the bond market is the largest financial market, why is it not discussed more on TV or in the news?" Bonds are not bought and sold in a real, open information market, like the stock market, where you have the moment-by-moment publicly available price of stocks that you can buy or sell. This does not happen in the normal bond market for average investors. Depending on who you are, how wealthy you may be, or who you know, you could be paying a higher or lower price for the exact same bond that someone else is buying. If you are just an average Joe investor, you will probably be paying the highest prices for your bond purchases.

Bond dealers and brokerages have "mark-up" fees for bond purchasers, with the mark-up fees reducing the bond's yield, which, over time, reduces the bond's return. Bond dealers may not tell you how much the mark-up fee is or how much the dealer/broker is making on its sale to you. Since 2018, brokers have been required to tell the public how much their mark-up of a bond is, but they do not have to give you that answer until after the transaction is finished. Most bonds are not traded like stocks which are bought and sold on public exchanges at current market prices. Bonds are traded "over the counter" among brokerage houses. The same type of bond can be sold at different prices to different people at the same time, depending on who is selling it, how many bonds are being bought, and who is buying it. Mark-ups range from 0.1% to 5% added to the bond par value. The higher the markup, the less yield you receive.

If you are rich and live in certain states, you can invest in triple tax-free Municipal Bonds that are usually exempt from Federal, state, and local taxes. You will generally pay no taxes on this income, but there are certain exemptions in different states. The greater income a person has, and the higher the tax bracket they are in, the more they can benefit from the advantages of holding Municipal Bonds. Wealth allows you the opportunity to hire the right advisors who can deliver greater economic opportunities that the lower and middle classes of our society do not have.

The best deal for buying U.S. Government Treasury bills, notes, and bonds is to open a personal United States Treasury Direct account. Your personal bank account is connected to your Treasury Direct Account, and you can place your orders to purchase Treasuries during an auction before the auction deadline, and on the settlement date, money will be automatically sent from your bank account to your Treasury Direct account. For one year or longer holdings you will receive an interest payment every six months that goes directly into your personal bank account. Many Treasury auctions are held weekly. You avoid any middlemen and paying commissions, and the interest you receive is exempt from state taxes.

BUYING VERSUS SAVING ECONOMICS

Government and business leaders and economists emphasize that what is good for both you and the American economy is for you to buy as much merchandise as you possibly can, and if you do not have the cash or money in your checking account, use your credit cards so you can buy more. These activities, they tell you, will make the United States more prosperous, and our country will have a stronger economy.

Here is something I have wondered about. How in the world did the people of this country survive and prosper before credit cards? In the 1950s and early 1960s, mostly only very well-off people had credit cards.

Around 1965-67, newer credit card companies started handing out credit cards with little in the way of thorough background checks of their new users. In high school, I worked during the summer at a men's clothing store, nowhere near where I lived. Every couple of days, we received big lists of people's names from these newer credit card companies who were either not paying their bills or using phony cards. Before we could run anyone's card, we had to first check the list.

Yet during the many years since the country's founding, when people used cash, gold or silver, or even just a handshake or IOU paper between buyers and sellers, America's economy grew and prospered. Today, credit card companies and banks seem to say that it is an American's duty to establish a good credit rating by using these cards from the time you are very young, so you can get into the card use habit, until one day, you find yourself with a half dozen or more cards and balances near the limit.

The advertising propaganda is that establishing creditworthiness will open doors for you; borrowing the money you don't have can get you a new car, bigger wedding rings, fancier clothes, more restaurant meals, and vacations anywhere. Just look at the ads that companies show on both TV and the Internet. "Hey, stranger, what's in your pocketbook? By-the-way, we may get hacked, and all your personal information might be floating in the black market of the Internet." Whoever thought of the idea that credit has anything to do with one's Karma? Maybe Confucius secretly wanted a credit card account. Having and using credit cards in general is the opposite of a FRAM oil filter advertisement. FRAM's slogan is "Pay me now or pay me later," which means that if you don't regularly change your car's oil and filter and use a FRAM filter, you may have huge automobile engine repairs or engine failures in the future.

Credit card companies tell you: "Don't pay all your bill now. Pay me a little bit now with high-interest rates. Then keep paying me minimum amounts with those added high-interest rates. Then, keep paying me and paying me forever. If you happen to die and your husband or wife is also on the credit card with them as a responsible user, they can keep paying me more." Why are people content to keep buying on credit, not paying their total credit card bills each month, and paying high-interest rates on those balances? Could it be not dealing with your addictive buying habits?

Unless you pay 100% of your monthly credit card bill, those high interest rates will increase the cost of whatever you owe while the value of the items you bought keeps decreasing over time. Even if you stop buying things with that credit card, the total amount of money you will have to pay to the credit card company will keep rising. So, over time, those $100 items may cost you around $150-200 because of the fees. Credit card interest rates are not like home mortgage interest rates. The home you bought might increase in value over time, while the items you bought with a credit card will either decrease in value or evaporate, like your restaurant bill. The food's gone, but the financial cost of the food you ate keeps rising.

So, here is an answer to my previous question: people are content because overusing a credit card is one of today's legal, behavioral addictions justified by "everyone else is doing it, so what's wrong with that?" People often use their credit cards to satisfy urges for immediate gratification. "I see, I want, I buy." It does not matter if you need the item; your wants become your needs. Behavior addictions cause problems, no matter what the thing, substance, or activity is: legal pharmaceutical drugs, illegal drugs, food, shopping, sex, pornography, alcohol, or doing whatever.

Once a person becomes a believer that having more of anything is better for them than not having or doing it, they fall into a self-created, justified behavioral pattern of addiction. These varieties of addictions do not follow logical thinking. Shooting heroin might be considered bad, but maybe shopping to the point where you cannot pay the bills that might result in a divorce, bankruptcy, or the loss of your home or car might not be considered bad. Maybe even the loss of being with your children is sort of okay because maybe it is happening to others you know. At least you are not a heroin junkie. You are just a shopping junkie, or an overeating junkie, or sex junkie. The behavioral patterns are all the same.

One of the TV channels, A&E, has a show called "Hoarders," which shows where addictive buying can take you. If you have no more room in your house, you start putting things in your garage. Then, no more room in the filled garage you need a pay-by-the-month storage locker, which advances to maybe getting another locker or a bigger storage locker: you are a hoarder. If you have a yard or open acreage, you have an ideal location for addictive buying to fill all the space you have.

Have you ever watched the TV show "American Pickers?" This show lets you watch both valuable artifacts and junk collectors. You can observe people who show great pride and order in their collections of antiques. Then there are those who have acres of rusted autos, tractors, building materials, scrap metal, or signs on their property, often buried in the soil. Sometimes, trees grow through and around them, displaying the many years since the object was originally placed there.

One aspect of this show that amazed me was seeing many men in their 70s and 80s unwilling to sell what they had collected. It was as if these objects were imagined to be made of gold or that they were like good friends, and parting with them was unthinkable. As with most types of hoarding behaviors, many hoarders do not seem to comprehend that when they die, they could be leaving a huge cleanup responsibility and task for someone else. If many objects are worth a lot of money, they can leave a nice inheritance for someone. If it's mostly junk, it can become a huge job that takes a lot of time, manpower, and money to resolve.

Hoarding can take many forms. I had a friend about 12 years older than me, and he was a money hoarder. He had sold a successful business at age 65, was collecting Social Security, and was now making $250,000 a year trading stock market options. He showed me his financial papers from a brokerage that listed his liquid assets at $8 million. Everything he owned was paid for. He and his wife had no children. He did not go on vacations nor take care of his health. The doctors had told him that if he moved to a better climate, he would live longer and be healthier. He did not move. He did not eat healthier or exercise more.

I had a discussion with him one day about his mounting fortune and not using some of it to benefit him and his wife more. He refused to answer that question specifically, but he told me that he was doing better than some of his friends. He mentioned that he had a 78-year-old friend who had $22 million in stocks and cash, and daily, this guy would go through local alleys looking into people's garbage dispensers for aluminum cans that he would take to places that pay you for your aluminum can returns. He said this guy was not an environmentalist, in fact, he said the guy was against the environmental movement. He did it for the money.

Hoarding and overspending are both behavioral addictions that can cause a lot of problems for anyone and their families. This Pandemic may have changed a lot of people's attitudes about credit card use and abuse, and these changes might produce more family stability and saving for emergencies or unexpected events. Maybe there will also be more positive changes in other behavioral addictions. Let us hope and pray for the best outcome. With inflation, people's debt loads are still increasing.

Unlike our American Government, we cannot print our own money. Instead of our politicians dealing with our country's national debt issues, they leave their governmental office and walk away with big pensions, leaving their debt responsibilities on the shoulders of future generations.

THE FEDERAL RESERVE

Back in the 1970s, there was a movie called "All the President's Men." The story was about the Watergate Investigation and President Nixon, his aides, and other Government officials involved in illegal activities, hidden money funds, and deceptions. The movie is based on the book with the same name written by Bob Woodward and Carl Bernstein. What was interesting to observe was the tactics these two reporters had used in trying to uncover the truth. Their Governmental source, called "Deep Throat," persisted in telling them they needed to ask the "right kind of questions of the right people" and "follow the money." If they followed this procedure, they might discover the answers that would lead to finding out what really happened.

Today, I listened to many reporters from different networks, all asking a government official the same question and receiving the same answer. I understand that it may be all about ratings reviews for the major news networks. The nightly news programs on ABC, CBS, and NBC are not places where viewers get many in-depth news stories explained, considering the broadcasts are only 30 minutes long with commercials. With Americans having such short attention spans, sitting and watching one news program for half an hour might be the extent to which many networks can keep news watchers paying attention. CNN, MSNBC, and FOX News are exceptions because they are continual news or entertainment channels showing dozens of commentators giving and interpreting news with opinions and biases, where every detail of a story is "breaking news."

Biases have gotten so ingrained into many of the news shows that truth no longer exists as something real. Many political leaders repeatedly lie because they know that by lying more to try and gain political favor among their cultish groupies, it is easier to convince them that everything they say is the truth, no matter how outrageous the lie may be. A tactic like this has been one of several precursors that have been used to establish totalitarian regimes throughout the history of the world.

Another curious aspect of how some reporters question an official is this: Why do reporters ask multiple questions in their supposed one question? Officials love this approach because they can then pick the easy question and go on with a time-consuming, rambling response, then blow off the other questions as they move on to another reporter. I wonder if reporters should take some debating classes where they could learn how to ask very specific questions, administered one at a time. More precise single questions may be helpful in getting more specific answers from government officials. How one phrases a question might make a huge difference in how officials respond.

Another thing that I have seen some reporters do, for example, is after a disaster of some type, where maybe a tornado or flood wiped out a person's home or several people were killed, they will ask a suffering person, "Well, how do you feel about this?" Come on, people, how do you think a person feels after a monstrous loss of property or someone's life? Why give sympathy and aid when breaking news helps ratings?

Usually, a different type of reporter covers events like the question-and-answer session after an announcement of actions taken by the Federal Reserve. These reporters seem more knowledgeable about economic issues concerning the business and financial world.

When Alan Greenspan was Chairman of the Federal Reserve of the United States from 1987-2006, he almost made a game of how he responded to reporters' questions. Greenspan was a real pro, a master of complicated wordings, and was called "The George Orwell of Corporate Doublespeak."

At a symposium in Jackson Hole, Wyoming, on August 26, 2005, sponsored by the Federal Reserve Bank of Kansas City, this is what Chairman Alan Greenspan said: "Any onset of increased investor caution elevates risk premiums and, as a consequence, lowers asset values and promotes the liquidation of the debt that supported higher asset prices." What?

Back then, after several of Greenspan's news conferences, which would involve a question-and-answer segment, people would walk out of the conference asking themselves, "What did he just say?"

The current Chairman of the Federal Reserve, Jerome Powell, now has news conferences after every major Fed Meeting during the year. These events are televised on the business channels, and the questioning audience is composed of reporters from businesses like The Wall Street Journal, CNBC, Bloomberg, and many other large information organizations that focus on business, banking, and the economy. One thing that stands out is that the average citizen in America is hardly represented in the audience of reporters. The focus seems to be mostly on major banks, brokerage companies, corporations, business interests outside the United States, and the richest investors. A major monetary focus is on how Fed decisions could or will benefit or hinder the top 1-10% of our citizens that hold most of the wealth. I have watched these Federal Reserve question-and-answer news conferences for many years, and there is almost no discussion of how the average citizen, especially seniors and conservative investors, is impacted by the decisions that are made by the Federal Reserve.

A lot of senior citizens and savers buy Treasury securities. The Federal Reserve controls short-term interest rates, and this influences the rates on the different types of securities they offer. Here is a simple list of some of the yields on 10-year U.S. Treasuries since 2000.

1-10-2000	6.69 %	1-13-2014	2.84 %
3-12-2001	4.78 %	1-26-2015	1.86 %
6-20-2005	3.92 %	7-18-2016	1.57 %
12-22-2008	2.16 %	10-15-2018	3.20 %
4-05-2010	3.90 %	10-04-2019	1.53 %
11-07-2011	1.93 %	2-28-2020	1.16 %
5-14-2012	1.71 %	3-02-2023	4.08 %

As the stock market dropped like a rock because of the initial fears of the COVID-19 pandemic in the spring of 2020, then bounced back to where it had started dropping early in the year, interest rates fell off a cliff. This is what the Federal Reserve wanted to happen: interest rates to be as close to zero as possible. Why? Because it helps the wealthiest investors who own most of the stock market's valuation. With these almost zero interest rates, stocks have more value, creating the potential for short -term stock speculation and quick escalating stock prices. Thus, the Federal Government, large speculators, and corporations could borrow huge sums of money with almost no interest. At the same time, Mom and Pop Average Americans continued to pay high-interest rates on their credit cards and received lower interest rates on mortgages, CDs, and bank accounts. Let's get back to those "question and answer" sessions with the Chairman of the Federal Reserve. When the Federal Reserve had driven interest rates down to about 0.00-0.25%, it was rare for any reporter in these meetings to ask this question: "Why do seniors and conservative investors have to suffer with declining incomes from vastly lower interest yields on their Treasury and CD purchases while the super-rich can use the same money to make riskier bets on stocks with minimal borrowing costs?" Government statistics show that in about twenty years, the 10-year Treasury went from a 6.7% yield in 2000 to a low 0.52% yield in 2020 while many major banks were only paying their depositors 0.01%.

In 2023, with higher inflation, the yield curve has inverted (higher interest for short-term treasury products, lower interest rates for longer- term products): you could get over 5% on a short-term CD. Great for consumers in one aspect, but not so hot if inflation is higher than 5%.

When The Federal Reserve makes drastic reductions in interest rates, and seniors lose income by investing and reinvesting in safer Treasuries, CDs, and bank accounts, these seniors and other conservative investors are called "collateral damage." An example of collateral damage might be a young child at home alone in an apartment building on a weekday playing with matches who accidentally set his parent's apartment on fire. In the process, other apartments caught fire and were destroyed or heavily damaged. These other apartments are collateral damage because of the child's actions. Their activity made other families suffer.

But with many types of products like food, gas, electricity, and medicines that seniors buy costing 5-10% more than a year or two ago, even with buying a 4-5% Treasury bill, inflation is eating away at their savings.

Many young and older stock advisors tell people, "Just invest in the stock market!" After what you have seen happen in the severe downward fluctuations in the stock market in 2022, 2020, and back in 2006-09, financial advisors still advise most people in their 80s or 90s to keep investing in stocks. These advisors tell people of all ages that stock investments will allow you to achieve wealth. Buy stocks, and when you are in your 70s, 80s, and 90s, you can sell your stocks and maybe make a lot of money. Of course, the definitive word here is "maybe." When you are a super senior, what would you rather have: possible wealth from wild stock market swings or financial security from stable, guaranteed-income sources? There is nothing safer than U.S. Government securities.

So, what is the deal with our Federal Reserve? How did they come into existence? In 1910, United States Republican leader Nelson Aldrich (whose daughter married John D. Rockefeller Jr.) secretly got together on Jekyll Island, Georgia, with Frank A. Vanderlip (also an associate of the Rockefellers) from National City Bank of New York, Henry Davison from J.P. Morgan Bank, Charles D. Norton from First National Bank of New York, Paul Warberg from Kuhn, Loeb, and Company, and Colonel Edward M. Huse to write up a plan to establish some type of a Reserve Bank. After several years of haggled discussions, President Woodrow Wilson signed the Federal Reserve Act into law on December 23, 1913.

In protest, Republican Representative Charles Lindberg Sr. of Minnesota told his colleagues: "But the Federal Reserve Board has no power whatever to regulate the rates of interest that bankers may charge borrowers of money. This is the Aldrich Bill in disguise, the difference being that by this bill the Government issues the money, whereas by the Aldrich Bill the issue was controlled by the banks…Wall Street will control the money as easily through this bill as they have heretofore."[55]

When we look out over the history of America's financial and business world, what might draw our attention? How about a bunch of super-rich dudes from the East Coast, mainly New York, getting together to write a plan to make themselves and their friends richer while leaving most of the lower and middle class behind?

What happened with the Financial Collapse from December 2007 to June 2009? A bunch of rich dudes, mainly associated with Wall Street and the banking industry in New York, got together and mostly bailed out the biggest United States banks and brokerage companies. At the same time, the poor and middle-class Americans lost their homes, savings, investments, and sanity while the super-rich were saved and became richer. Forward to December 2017, when the Tax Cuts and Jobs Act was passed. This was proposed by a super-rich real estate executive from New York, then President of the United States. What did this legislation do? The big picture: employment went up, with average Americans seeing about a 3-5% rise in yearly income. Did the super-rich see a 3-5% rise in income? Of course not. Their incomes increased by 15, 20, or 30%, which increased income inequality even more. Then came the pandemic. Unemployment skyrocketed to nearly 20% in the spring of 2020, then started dropping.

The official jobs unemployment rate for June 2020 was 10.1% for white workers, 15.4% for black workers, and 14.5% for Hispanic workers, and the number of Americans unemployed was very high. The following is a statement given by Federal Reserve Chairman Powell to a U.S. Senate Banking Committee in June 2020: "Any economic rebound will take a long time to reach all corners of the job market…Already disadvantaged groups are likely to suffer the most. Low-income households have experienced, by far, the sharpest drop in employment, while job losses of African

Americans, Hispanics, and women have been greater than that of other groups. If not contained and reversed, the downturn could further widen gaps in economic well-being."[56] Gaps in economic well-being are another way of saying income inequality.

Years ago, yearly gains from the stock market were averaging around 6-12%, while fixed income saw gains of 3-7%. Over the last number of decades of seeing wild swings both up and down, stock market investor expectations have risen to levels where they want or expect 20-30% or higher yearly gains from their investments. A new attitude has developed for many 20-50-year-old investors. "For me, it is not about being well off in retirement: it's about becoming super rich before I'm 50 or 55, not when I'm 65, 70, or 75. Spend and live life to its fullest when you are young, buy whatever you want, think big, act big, and live for today. Saving and looking forward to the future is a dead-end journey." Party hearty!

It is this changed investing attitude that encourages greater economic separation between the top 10% of the population and everyone else. Many "newly rich" Americans either inherited wealth from their family and had a good chunk of available funds to get in on the early start of investing in certain tech companies or crypto, or those who, through friends or family, were able to receive inside information on company or government dealings silently. All these groups feel that they are the chosen ones who deserve a carefully delineated separation of wealth-building opportunities over anyone outside of their social and economic class.

Over the years, this has created more walled-off, gated communities where they can afford the privilege to live whatever bodacious lifestyles they choose, which grants them separation from everyone else.

Many rich people feel that being wealthy is a right, not a privilege. They feel that their massive wealth accumulation entitles them to receive greater advantages over other people. They can manipulate financial and business markets to create avenues of success not available to people in other economic classes. It is not through physical work that they achieve their successes; it is from the creative thinking of their employees and their wealth connections that greater wealth is achieved. Remember Adam Smith: it takes 500 poor people to make one rich.

America has become a plutocracy where the rules and regulations are made by a Congress of individuals with great wealth and social standing in their states. This change in governing automatically gives our Congress the ability to favor rich individuals and corporations who have donated the greatest amounts of money to their political campaigns. This activity often keeps politicians winning many elections and staying in office for decades. Many politicians think their power positions are so important that they try to stay in office until they no longer possess the ability to talk or understand what is going on with generations of people in their states who are fifty to seventy years younger than themselves.

Many modern-day politicians would rather follow extremist leaders who spread negative cultish propaganda for power and popularity rather than exhibiting the ethics and morals that our Founding Fathers used to create our country.

Look around America. We are emotionally and psychologically distancing ourselves from each other, creating the greatest separation in wealth and politics since the Civil War. With the current political system, the rich get vastly richer while the middle and lower classes get left behind. Read the history of what happens to nations when similar situations occur. Maybe we need another revolution to get our country to recenter its priorities. Maybe it's time to elect new, younger, more common, average people to guide us: people who might better understand what average middle and lower classes of people are going through. So, where do we go from here?

Are you going to continue voting for those politicians who exhibit extreme bias toward their rich friends and corporations, or will you vote for those who advocate cooperation and compassion for everyone? Let's call it choosing people over party. This is what President George Washington advocated when he left office.

Chapter 7

EDUCATION FOR LIFE: THEN AND NOW

"What the vast majority of American children need is to stop being pampered, stop being indulged, stop being chauffeured, stop being catered to. In the final analysis, it is not what you do for your children but what you have taught them to do for themselves that will make them successful human beings."[57] (Ann Landers)

Looking around the country today, you might see what Ann Landers is talking about. I call it "parental-created, spoiled children." The real troubling aspect of Landers' words is that she said them in 1968.

The educational system in the United States is failing both our students and the country. Our politicians brag about our stock market, billionaires, mega-mansion-sized homes, technical advances, Internet pioneers (Google, Facebook, etc.), military power, and merchandising and marketing delivery systems like Amazon and Walmart. They brag about certain colleges and graduate schools, the size of university stadiums, and sporting achievements. But I do not hear people brag about the world rankings of our K through 12th-grade school students.

We cannot brag because the U.S. ranks nowhere near the top. Our grade school and high school students' educational comprehension levels are some of the worst among industrialized societies. The U.S. spends more money per student than any other country in the world, with only mediocre results.

Do the physical accomplishments of our students in football, basketball, and baseball create more knowledgeable, educated, and aware citizens, or do they just produce better fullbacks and quarterbacks, dribblers and shooters, or hitters and pitchers? Sports are promoted among our students as an avenue for potentially becoming "professional athletic successes" and helping to advance their school's sports reputation and name recognition throughout the region, state, or country.

Instead of schools becoming more well-known for developing highly perceptive, exceptionally educated students, many schools have become more like professional sports teams. Their local fans become more like "stockholders," full-season ticket holders who use mass marketing booster clubs to buy and sell school logo merchandise, creating even more funding for their sports programs.

The educational opportunities available for many elementary and high school students are unbalanced and unfair across the education spectrum throughout the United States. Some of our school systems may have great teachers, fully equipped classrooms, and labs with the latest technological learning devices. Yet, another school system 5-50 miles away may have the barest minimums of these same facilities with outdated books, insufficient libraries, molding infrastructures, broken equipment, and second-rate teachers.

Statewide educational opportunities for students range from the best locally available to the worst. This will almost guarantee the perpetuation of a local education and social structure of "haves and have-nots," especially when local governmental taxes mainly fund school systems. Wouldn't a more fair and balanced approach to achieve statewide equal education for all students be to collect all the statewide school taxes meant for education, divide that amount by the number of students in the state, and allocate that amount for each student to the school system where they are located?

In this way, you are treating all students the same and not picking winners and losers. Wouldn't this be the "democratic" way to do things? Why is a system like this not used today?

It is not done this way because the educational system in the United States is run based on aristocratic delineations. Don't let any politician fool you; many systems in both government and industry operate through an aristocratic format. Let's say you live in a lower-class economic area next to a petrochemical plant and want to talk to your United States Senator or State Governor about the negative effects your children face from the poor air quality around your home. Try to get an appointment to speak one-on-one with this government person. Being an industrialist who either wants to build another chemical plant nearby or who wants to give that politician a generous campaign contribution will allow them to see the official any time of any day. Politicians are "bought" by corporations through campaign fund donations, corporate junkets, or by being taken to fancy restaurants and exotic travel locations.

Treating politicians like they are aristocrats sets up a framework of greater delineation between social classes and should not be allowed in a democratic republic. In America, money and power create privileges unavailable to poor parents and children whose poor health is then ignored.

Here in the United States, there is an educational system where the amount of money spent on each pupil is about the same, the quality of education is excellent, and in certain areas, more comprehensive and advanced than any of the average school systems in America. It is called the United States Military.

Military training and educational facilities exist all over the country, and it does not matter if your parents are multimillionaires, on welfare, or donating money to politicians. You get a great education that produces not only well-educated graduates but also individuals who are disciplined and healthy, in contrast to what is currently going on with the high obesity rates of our children, teenagers, and college students. Why can't a similar type of approach be used for regular school venues?

I am not suggesting we turn our schools into military institutions. Certain aspects of military education develop positive health and etiquette behaviors, discipline, and philosophies that inspire enthusiasm, devotion, and a personal sense of honor for all participants. This type of training would not include how to kill or harm others, how to blow things up, how to disable people, or how to dominate others mentally or physically.

A semi-standardization of clothing is currently used by some school systems in various countries and many locales around the world, as well as in numerous Catholic and public schools in America. Why not use it nationwide? After school hours, you can wear whatever you want. Obviously, the fashion industry would not like this approach, but the fashion industry does not have the job or responsibility of educating our children.

The costs of fashionable clothing and the words of braggadocious garment wearers in schools can easily develop into bullying, separation barriers, degrading language used against other students, and jealousies. Over the years, the somewhat false "clothing makes the student unique" beliefs and ideologies have been pointed out in hundreds of movies, TV commercials, and the Internet. Is one of a school's primary purposes to educate our children on how to out-dress each other for image and status?

Another aspect of receiving a military education is training one's body using our natural circadian rhythm patterns, which make the body and the mind function at a higher level. Physically trained students are less obese, have fewer diseases and malfunctioning organs, and they are more likely to be happier. But maybe parents do not want these positive aspects for their children. Maybe they just want their children to be copies of themselves with whatever is going on with their own personal health.

Maybe instead of tired, "zombie-like" children who fall asleep or cannot pay attention in class because of lack of sleep or too much electronic gadget stimulation, this country could refocus on what is essential to produce higher student retention levels. Not only will students have a better understanding of facts and figures, but also a greater awareness and responsibility for their physical health and personal outlook on life.

Our Founding Fathers participated in various methods to self-educate and discipline themselves by using logic, common sense, and appreciation, which they eventually formulated into our laws and rights based on religious morals and ethics. They educated themselves to learn about a variety of historical and philosophical movements, how various types of govern-ments around the world ruled their citizens, and what happened to societies ruled by dictators and monarchs. They used scholarship to investigate what were some of the best methods for governing the citizens. Do we follow in their footsteps, or do we allow lying politicians and the internet's lack of morals and ethics to be our inspirations in how we formulate our coun-try's educational guidance?

STORY BY RUTH: HER EARLY LIFE

This is a real-life story written by an acquaintance who died about thir-teen years ago at 97. I recently discovered her story and felt it was appro-priate to share it in this book. No wording, punctuation, or sentence struc-ture was changed.

"When the Depression began, I was 17 years old, preparing to graduate from high school the following year. My parents quickly lost their business of selling and servicing radios from the basement of our home, employing my father and brother. My brother was fortunate to find temporary em-ployment on the assembly line of an automobile manufacturer, and my father was able to work on the WPA (Works Progress Administration), repairing sidewalks, etc. There was no welfare program or unemployment insurance, but the government allowed those buying their homes to pay only the interest.

This made it possible for us to keep our home, for which we were very grateful. My mother got up very early in the morning to make sandwiches which my father sold to those working with him on the WPA projects. The high school graduating class could not afford caps and gowns; girls wore white dresses and the boys wore suits. Aunt Lee kindly sewed a white dress for me so that I could graduate, and purchased a yearbook for me. The class ring and pictures were not affordable.

I was awarded the Gold Medal for having the highest grades in the Commercial Course. As a reward, another Aunt paid for additional train-ing in Davis Business College, where I finished the course quicker than anyone before me. There was a $35 rebate, which I was allowed to spend for a class in the use of the Comptometer, which much later enabled me to take a two-year wartime job in Detroit. Davis Business College allowed those who graduated to continue attending classes, free of charge, until they could place us in jobs.

In a short time, I was offered a job in a law firm where I worked for five years before leaving to marry. I was first hired on a temporary basis at $10 a week. A few weeks later the job was permanent at $12 a week and increased soon to $15. We worked six days a week, from 9 to 5, with no overtime pay. We were paid twice a month, so the pay was not truly $15 a week; we received $30 on payday. A few years later I pointed this out, and received a true $18 a week, when I was secretary to the senior lawyer. At one point we only worked half days on Saturday.

I purchased family drug needs (soap, etc.) and my brother helped with food. No meals were ever eaten out except my lunches, which I limited to not over 30 cents.

I rode the streetcar to work except when a neighbor or friend gave me a ride. I was lucky to get nice hand-me down clothes, which really helped because we were expected to make a good appearance. The bank closings caused great difficulty, and it was years before I received the last of my childhood savings of about $25. On the plus side, it certainly taught us the value of money, and it took many, many years for us to be the least bit frivolous in our spending, and we never lost the habit of always looking for the best prices and seeking bargains." By Ruth.

Ruth came from an average American family, not a historically poor family. Just think for a second what it must have been like if your family was already poor when the Depression started.

Chapter 8

HAPPINESS AND THE MAGIC MIRROR

"Happiness doesn't depend upon who you are or what you have, it depends on what you think." Dale Carnegie

Some people get absorbed into defining "happiness" by using a materialistic framework. Yet there are many areas of the world where people have fewer possessions than the average American citizen, but those less materially privileged seem to be a lot happier. Americans do not want to focus on what is going on materialistically and emotionally with those other people because we cannot seem to justify how they can be happier with less. That very idea is anathema to what Americans are taught by parents, teachers, corporations, and politicians to believe and follow.

What do many parents tell their children when viewing pictures or movies of societies that have less or very little materialism in their lives? "Do you want to be like those people? They are poor and look at how little they have, rags for clothes, with some running around half naked. You would not be able to watch your favorite TV shows or use your cell phone. We are raising you to be successful." A lot of people must think that success and owning a great number of objects are keys to one's happiness. Have you ever stopped to really look at the so-called poorer people in Africa, South or Central America, or Asia and wondered: "Why are these children all smiling and happy when my children don't act like that unless I buy them some pricey technological gadget or toy every week or two?"

Inner happiness is not measured by the size of bank accounts, the number of toys a child has, one's stock portfolio, or the type of car you drive. Happiness is defined by concepts like peace of mind, gratefulness to be alive, having close family and trusted friend relationships, being healthy in body and mind, and having an attitude that loves mankind while acknowledging the awe and the wonders of nature.

Biblically, Christ lived for several decades before he preached and was crucified. Do you think he whined and complained about not having enough material possessions as a child or young adult?

When you live with a "more is better" psychological approach toward materialism, does your happiness depend on satisfying all your wants? Will great sums of money automatically give you a happy heart and soul? Will it give you emotional peace of mind? Will it make your behavioral addictions disappear?

On the contrary, striving for more and more materialistic wealth will probably increase your addictive behaviors. Do you think that most people really care about their addictive behaviors? The trend toward owning more of everything created by their greater addictive behaviors seems to be increasing. Look at all the negative reactionary behaviors that went on during the COVID-19 pandemic because people had to deal with less than their normal status quo of social interactions and material accumulation.

It was our addictive behaviors that caused the spread of the virus to increase geometrically because of our social addictions to closely gathering with others and partying with food feasts, alcohol, or illegal drugs. "Loose lips sink ships," a terminology used in propaganda posters during World War II, meant "beware of unguarded talk in public" about military or government matters you might know about. The unmasked talking behavior near others during the Pandemic killed a lot of people. During many Covid days, it was the air and moisture coming from our lips that infected, medically disabled, or maybe killed your parents or grandparents who may have had weaker immune systems.

Today's modern culture "tends to reinforce the things that don't work in trying to create our happiness," according to Ronald Siegel PsyD, assistant clinical professor of psychology at Harvard Medical School/Cambridge Health Alliance. "It fools us into thinking (happiness is) all about these external matters" and "we don't have very many messages that point us to a different direction for finding happiness." The constant search for happiness creates a "hedonic treadmill. We become accustomed to what we have and need more and more to feel good."[58]

Dr. Siegel advises us to stop getting lost in our thoughts about what we do today and what happened yesterday. He mentions that the resulting happiness does not last long if we do something just for ourselves. This fits in with the "Capitalism for Me" perspective and why the accumulation of more possessions over time does not necessarily mean lasting happiness follows.

The greatest psychological minds or therapies will never solve your behavioral addictions unless you recognize them in yourself first. Take some time to watch young children interact with each other before they get old enough to begin absorbing the "ego lingo" propaganda that parents and others start telling them. From whom did children hear ideas like: "It's mine, not yours; we're better than them; they are not the right color; my father is more important and makes more money than yours?"

Before parental or caretaker biases are spoken to young children, these same children have no problem accepting each other as equals, regardless of their color, race, or parental asset values.

If we continually remind ourselves and others that the search for happiness is achieved by what we own and what more we can accumulate during our lives, we may wind up satisfying our wants but lose our souls in the process.

The following is a short summary from an article by Jenna Lowthert describing her view of how to achieve happiness in 10 easy steps. Those steps are: Ignore the opinions of others, know your worth, do what you love and love what you do, express gratitude, let go of anger, live in the moment, pay it forward, be yourself, be honest, and smile." [59]

Suppose your happiness is defined by the technological flashing images on screens. If the music you listen to, texts you receive from friends or companies on your cell phone, the "likes" you get from social media sites, or what you can buy in stores or online, creates your happiness, imagine what would happen if a foreign government or terrorist group created a long-term power grid failure? Your psychological withdrawals could be similar to those experienced by heroin, meth, or cocaine junkies.

MIRROR, MIRROR, WHO AM I?

One of the things that I am hoping to achieve with this book is for you, a rich, poor, or middle-income American citizen, to take a short block of your time and spend it looking into a mirror. Examine yourself in depth. Are you as physically healthy as you would like to be? Mentally and emotionally healthy? Are any of your behaviors harmful to yourself and could those behaviors negatively impact the way you treat others? This type of mirror work is generally not a "one-and-done" exercise for your mind. For some people, there can be a single day of revelation. For most people, though, change is a process that may take months or years. That mirror will always be there for you, no matter how long it takes.

It is often very difficult to get people to do mirror work because this type of activity often makes us see aspects of ourselves that we might have intentionally forgotten. Or it generates memories so deeply buried within us that we do not want to bring them back because they may make us feel uncomfortable.

What we are suppressing may be what's creating instability in our thought processing. It could be events from our childhood that involved pain or abuse, bullying or being bullied, a divorce, a family tragedy, sexual misconduct against us, a war experience, or as basic as the loss of a pet. You may have buried an event or series of events because you did not want to ever deal with those memories again. Keeping them deeply buried seemed to you to be the wisest choice at the time, but if you experienced severe trauma, you may wish to seek professional counseling.

When you look into a mirror, you need to look beyond the physical image you are seeing. Look beyond the clothes, the make-up, the hairstyle, and the social image you have created for yourself. Look within your heart and mind. Look at the mistakes you have made during your life and the bad habits or actions that created discomfort for yourself or others. Look at the consequences of those choices. Have your actions or inactions caused others grief, sorrow, loss of home, jobs, or investments?

Have your physical or emotional addictions to drugs, foods, sex, money, power, or control caused problems for yourself, your family, or your country? Maybe you are in denial about the consequences of your own life's history. Try not to be a: "It's the f--king past, man, who gives a shit" responder. That very line may be an attitudinal aspect of why life is not going the way you would like.

Reading how our traveling pioneers during the 1800s, our soldiers in both World Wars, or how people dealt with adversity during the Depression and Dust Bowl of the 1930s may make your problems not sound so overwhelming. Millions and millions of individual people and families in our country have overcome huge obstacles and forged ahead to lead happy, moral, and ethical lives. (For an eye-opening experience, watch the Ken Burns PBS documentary "The Dust Bowl" from 2012.)

Another avenue to explore is sharing your thoughts and feelings with your parents or grandparents about what problems, adversities, or discriminations they may have encountered. Learning how they reacted or solved their own issues might give you valuable insights into your own life.

 So much is going on around us these days that it is easy to feel overwhelmed. These external events can often disrupt our innate moral and ethical compass to the point that we feel lost, confused, and depressed.

Heavily participating in social networking can often give you an overdose of both subject matter and emotional stress for your mind to digest. More of anything never automatically means better. Downtime is necessary for our well-being but is often negated in economic circles.

Remember the learned awareness of what the movie "Groundhog Day" was trying to tell us. When your life's history keeps repeating itself, you will only escape the negative recurrences by changing your perceptions and focusing on what you are doing and feeling in the present that is causing your problems. Today is the best day to create a new outlook.

There is much we can learn from the lives of our parents and grandparents. Much of the garbage and innuendo that is placed on social media sites today would not have been tolerated by those Americans who lived through the Great Depression, fought in World War II, and built the infrastructure of the 1940s and 50s. Back then most people believed in the importance and necessity of compromise. People focused on trying to achieve what was best for the hard-working middle class of America. Parents taught their children that there was more to life than just making money. As was daily displayed on the TV shows of the 1950s and early 1960s, having a fulfilling life incorporating love, kindness, generosity, and forgiveness in one's dealings with others is often more satisfying than just focusing on and striving for greater wealth accumulation.

Today, we are making many of our personal life choices based on following the advice of a specific leader who is constantly telling us to follow him because he says he knows what is best for our state or country. This pattern of propaganda is historically how dictators take over nations. Allowing ourselves to participate in a "group think" camaraderie creates a dependence on the views and attitudes of others to fill the voids we have self-created by abstaining from using our own rationalizing abilities. We start functioning as pawns on life's chessboard, moving straight forward, like pawns, toward goals prescribed for us by the bishops, knights, and queens of the political, social media, and commercial empires. By siding with them, they can then control every aspect of what they want us to believe is best for our individual lives.

Maybe we should stop being who we would like to be and just start being who we are. Do you feel your life is boring because you are not experiencing it like a movie star, a popular singer, a super athlete, or a billionaire? When people set their life at maximum speed, they zoom past many important feelings and insights that are important for them to understand. What has been discarded or abandoned may have been the exact solutions we needed.

While zooming through life, we can also lose our ability to make more common-sense decisions in our interactions with people and institutions. In many ways, today's modern technology is "stupefying" us. Instead of using historical reasoning and self-analysis to understand and help us deal with the significant events occurring around us, we use programmed electronic gadgets and platformed propaganda to influence our decisions about what to think, believe, and how to behave as we age.

We do not seem to be employing the methods that Our Founding Fathers used to educate themselves, by adopting the wisdom and virtues of great philosophers and scientists who inspired them to develop the foundation for our United States.

Today, we seem to feel that our advanced technology has made us smarter than ever before. Yes, Americans were smart enough in 2022 to lose $2.7 billion in investment scams, $3.7 billion in cryptocurrency scams, $40 billion in computer phishing phone scams, and 460,000 check fraud cases. The statistics for 2023 and 2024 show even greater losses. Then there are identity thefts, data breaches, ransomware attacks, denial of service attacks, data alteration problems, and others. We are repeatedly told that today's new high technology is making our lives simpler, safer, and easier every year. "Let the machines handle it," say our new horizon technologists, "and you will be happier and wealthier in the future." If that is the case why is it that in today's reality, people feel more confused, angrier, and unhealthier while living from paycheck to paycheck, hoping that some aristocratic, capitalistic, wannabe isolationist will solve all their problems and relieve them from all the physical and mental pressures they are now experiencing?

Philosopher George Santayana said, "Those who cannot remember the past are condemned to repeat it."

Chapter 9

INTROSPECTION OR US VERSUS THEM

There are three things going on right now in our American society that, if they continue for another decade, could cause a further disintegration of our great country. The three things that might cause our self-destruction are obesity and negative addictive behaviors, the growing trend of decadence with an "I want it all, I want it now"[60] social approach toward life, and the collapse of moral and ethical values in our relationships with other countries, ourselves, our families, and each other.

It will not be the lack of military strength that will cause the downfall. No one is going to invade the United States. That is a suicide mission for any potential invader who would need at least 20 to 30 million invading troops covering the country to maintain some type of control. Americans have more guns and armaments than it has citizens. (But passive and naïve citizens might allow cyber criminals to destroy our infrastructure.)

Citizens would not face the invaders directly but through internal rebellion: military and civilian trained sharpshooters killing invaders from long distances, massive car bombs, or Americans destroying or crippling the infrastructure to prevent use by the invaders. Look at other examples in history. Both the French and Americans failed in Vietnam. The Americans and Russians failed in Afghanistan. Like the Greeks, the Old Roman

Empire failed in the external areas they invaded. Hitler and Napoleon failed in Russia, and England failed in America.

We may or may not fail because of right-wing, extremist, conservative thinking or left-wing, extremist, liberal, or socialist thinking. With the trend toward tribalism becoming so strong, maybe some people think that the country would be better off being divided into "faction areas" where we live within our tribes. Liberals here, conservatives over there, LGBTQ in another area, atheists in one section, Evangelical Christians in another. If you want to know how that would work out, read "Adjustment Day" by Chuck Palahniuk, which probes dividing the country into tribal areas, each with its own social and cultural prejudices.

Is a bug or disease, like COVID-19, going to "take us out?" It is possible if we keep behaving in many states as we did during the pandemic's height, but I'm betting against it. How about a ruler getting too powerful, too rich, too authoritarian, along with a Congress who sides with that ruler? Chances are he could eventually be "taken out" by some non-believer who is fanatical and freaks out in a mental meltdown.

No, it will be a combination of the three reasons I originally chose. It would be somewhat subtle, slowly occurring over time, as it is now, with leaders using political correctness to ignore it until it may be too late. Only great political, economic, and social changes that mainly focus on the needs of the average Joe might return us to the Founding Fathers' morals, ethics, and inspirational ideologies.

For a couple of minutes, let's think about what type of government and society you prefer. First, we have the current situation: "Capitalism for Me" put together by corporations and corporate lobbyists who are privately associated with Congressional politicians who set up and enforce or don't enforce their own rules, regulations, and philosophies. The richest people keep getting vastly richer as they distance themselves from people who are just surviving by living paycheck to paycheck or a group where some are doing a little better, and the last group who always seem to be living in poverty. We have a college education system where you borrow huge sums of money for an education that economic propagandists tell you is necessary if you want to succeed. We have a tax system where the rich get loopholes that protect specialized income with lower tax rates, which gives them greater advantages to make millions and billions. Most people with normal incomes do not get these opportunities.

We have a health care system that favors the insurance companies and pharmaceutical companies over those average Americans who keep paying higher insurance rates while getting less care in their attempts to solve their health problems while trying to avoid bankruptcy. How much are you willing to be taxed to receive free health care, higher quality health maintenance facilities, inexpensive drugs, less income inequality, greater happiness, and more personal freedom? Look at the choices Finland has made.

Our government wastes hundreds of billions of dollars on pet political and corporate projects. Billions of dollars disappear from failed audits at the Department of Defense and other Government branches. Money is handed out like candy for cost overruns in corporate contracts. Wouldn't you think this money could be better used to help take care of average citizens' health? So far, it does not seem your voting choices of who you feel should be leading the Government are doing a great job. Maybe this last or the next election will change things, but maybe your tribalism will maintain the status quo.

Let us return to the three self-destructive factors mentioned at the beginning of this chapter. Number one: obesity and negative addictive behaviors.

I know what some of you might be thinking. This author is probably some skinny, bearded, left-wing radical who has no idea what life is like for us obese or overweight people with many health problems. I have a picture of my brother and me at a beach in grade school, standing next to each other, wearing bathing suits. My brother was one grade behind me in school. In that picture, I am more than twice my brother's size. My so-called grade school friends that I played with would often ridicule me because of my size and weight.

One day, I had enough of that talk and knew I needed to change my life, so I started vigorously riding my single speed bicycle. Back then, we couldn't afford multi-speed bikes to easily go up and down hills; it was one speed or walking. My friends periodically had one-on-one running races against each other after school hours. One day, after a couple of months of biking like a madman, I entered one of those running races. I beat every kid except the fastest kid in my group. I did not need to run in any more races because I had proved a point to my friends and myself.

By the time I left high school, during which I did a couple of years of self-instructed weight training, aerobic exercises, and monitoring my diet, I graduated very physically fit and in the best shape of my life. In the first semester of my first year in college, I was hit by a car, which broke or damaged several areas of my body, including my head and face.

I was unconscious for numerous days, and my parents had a priest administer my "last rites" because the doctors had told them that they did not think I was going to make it. I owe my survival to how I trained and conditioned my body during those high school years.

I have written about obesity and overeating in another chapter, but I would like to add a few discussion points here. The more people overeat and become obese, the greater the negative impact this activity will have on maintaining the strength and vitality of our nation and our standing in the world. Being obese can create many detrimental side-effects within your body.

1. CANCER
2. HIGH BLOOD PRESSURE
3. DIABETES
4. OSTEOARTHRITIS
5. GALLBLADDER DISEASE AND GALLSTONES
6. BREATHING PROBLEMS - SLEEP APNEA AND ASTHMA

Not every obese person will have all these problems, but if you have a family history with family members having one or more of these medical complications, your chances greatly increase. Dealing with these issues takes time, money, and doctor and therapist appointments and higher insurance rates for everyone. What do your children think when they see a parent's health falling apart? Maybe a more critical perspective is: how do parents feel when they see their children's health falling apart as a youth, teen, or person in their 20s from obesity or other health issues connected to obesity? Is it not the parent's responsibility to care for, raise, and guide a child from birth to adulthood? Is that not what parenting means? When many members of any society start falling apart because of serious health issues, it weakens one of the foundations of a nation's strength: the physical welfare and happiness of the populace.

The overconsumption of food is not the only type of legally addictive behavior that can harm an individual, the family, and the nation. How about addictive shopping, gambling, hoarding, destructive relationships, sex, pornography, and video games?

In an article published in the International Journal of Preventive Medicine, S.S. Alavi and associates state: "Behavioral addiction and substance addiction have a high rate of co-occurrence, suggesting the two conditions may share a common cause. The two addictions have similar mechanisms of action on the brain. Both substance abuse and engaging in addictive behaviors target the brain's reward system and produce feelings of pleasure…A person may be diagnosed with a behavioral addiction if they show loss of self-control over the behavior, including continuation of the behavior despite negative consequences in work or social relationships."[61]

Individuals do not like to be told to change their behaviors. For them to give up any legal addictive behavior is not consistent with what their egos and desires are telling them. "Why should I stop? It's legal, isn't it?" The end consequences of their behavior may negatively influence and ruin not only themselves but their family and friends. Today's governmental authorities do not seem too interested in doing much about many of these behavioral addictions, especially in our nation's children.

The second self-destructive factor is the decadent thinking that "More is Always Better."

Some people believe there are some limitations on the availability of natural resources. Through the last several centuries in the United States, many indigenous peoples approached nature with great respect, care, and conservation of the land and water, but these people were labeled savages, uncivilized, worthless Indians. Political leaders of both parties secluded these people on reservations, with the physical settings having minimal, if any, natural resources on which these people could survive. The Indians' previous homelands had gold, crude oil, buffalo, trapping areas for animal furs, and fields rich for growing crops. What good were those lands for the uncivilized Indian when Mr. White Man had the tools and knowledge to make profits from the land by growing more food and killing the natural-ranging animals?

Then, when those animals were all dead, the land was used to grow more food to feed and breed livestock for mass slaughterhouses. Everything was done to make more money and create greater power. More chemical fertilizers and toxic insecticides were sprayed on the land, which polluted our streams, lakes, and rivers, combined with manure residue. This was the "new technology" of the day. Grow more, eat more, pollute more, make more money – more is better.

Whether you look back a hundred years or just look at what goes on today, who were the people who primarily advocated these philosophies both then and now? It was the same 1%-10% of the wealthiest people in the country who were not satisfied with the then millions, now billions of dollars they made. After all, these people are our superior aristocrats endowed by God to be the "cream of the crop" of our society. They invent the major guidance and beliefs that everyone else is told to follow.

The philosophical belief that "more is better" creates a natural decadence in our society because it amplifies both extreme conservative and extreme liberal thinking. It is not middle-of-the-road attitudes, philosophies, and beliefs that create decadence. Living a life of compromise, fairness, understanding, and shared equality among the population creates greater harmony for the entire nation. Extremes create conflict and strife.

What are some of today's extremes? Don't get just a few tattoos; tattoo both arms, maybe your entire body. Don't just change the basic color of your hair; make it multi-colored; the more colors, the better. Don't kill one or two people at a time; killing lots of people makes you more famous. Why accidentally use a four-letter word when you can intentionally use the word in every sentence you speak and raise your popularity among your fans? As a national leader, why tell a couple of fibs when you can lie thousands of times, and your base will love you even more? Why only have sex with your husband or wife, girlfriend or boyfriend, when you can have sex with anyone at any time, even with someone you don't even know who's on your computer screen, or a totally lifelike doll you had specially made to your preferences that cost you a bundle of money to make?

Let's talk about sex. According to the "Sexually Transmitted Disease Surveillance Report" from the United States Centers for Disease Control and Prevention, published in October 2019, for the fifth year in a row, the combined cases of gonorrhea, chlamydia, and syphilis in the United States had risen to a total of 2.4 million infections that were diagnosed and reported in the last year, the highest number ever recorded.

Dr. Gail Bolan, director of the CDC's Division of STD Prevention, wrote: "Yet not that long ago, gonorrhea rates were at historic lows, syphilis was close to elimination, and we were able to point to advances in STD prevention. That progress has since unraveled. The number of reported syphilis cases is climbing after being largely on the decline since 1941. Many young women continue to have undiagnosed chlamydial infections, putting them at risk for infertility."

Elizabeth Torrone, a CDC epidemiologist, said: "STDs cause a significant burden to the health care system – both in terms of direct medical costs for treating STDs as well as the personal cost for people who have an STD." This CDC Report also said that teens and young adults 15-24 acquire 50% of all new STD cases, with 1 in 4 sexually active adolescent girls having an STD.[62]

You may be telling yourself the following: "Just have everyone vaccinated for these three deadly STDs." Research this statement, and you will find there are no vaccines for syphilis, gonorrhea, or chlamydia.

Extremism, today, has become the "norm." When an extreme behavior like lying becomes the norm, the truth becomes a lie, and the lie becomes the truth. Throughout history, this is the same form of propaganda that created the rise of Hitler types. If a country's leader or their representatives repeat the lies often enough, the public eventually believes them to be the truth. Leaders will explain that only they can make a country's population more affluent, put more people to work, and make the country stronger in its military and economic standing compared to the rest of the world. What they proclaim and how they will achieve it is not relevant.

When people look around society and observe greater decadent behaviors, they can irrationally justify their own behavior as "my truth." "This is what I am. My tribal truths tell me my behaviors are in line with my friends and associates. Who are you, an outsider, to question what I do, what I say, how I dress, who I have sex with, or who gets my vote?" This is a classic addictive behavior, and the denials reinforce and justify that behavior.

Historically, our parents and grandparents have been the role models that children and young adults look to as inspirational examples of goodness and well-being. Have many of these same role models now become the social has-beens who cannot understand the newer technological lifestyles and the freedom to want and have it all right now instead of in the future? This is what often occurs when addictive behaviors become typical mainstream, extremist lifestyles. More me, less we.

The last self-destructive factor is the collapse of moral and ethical values. Morals and ethics are part of the foundation of having and practicing historical common sense in our daily lives. Think back to the Old Testament and the New Testament. It is not the Biblical stories that are significant, but the moral and ethical guidelines demonstrated in the stories that show how people should relate to each other. These guidelines became the framework of Christianity and other faiths.

Our Founding Fathers used these guidelines to establish the foundational pillars by which good government could flourish for the betterment of the people in trying to achieve their pursuit of happiness.

There are those that might complain about what was just mentioned. "I thought there is supposed to be a separation between religion and government in the United States?" Yes, there is a "separation of church and state." The "Establishment Clause" and the "Free Exercise Clause" of the First Amendment to the United States Constitution say: "Congress shall make no law respecting an establishment of religion or prohibiting the free exercise thereof."

In 1952, the United States Supreme Court, in Zorach vs. Clauson, upheld "accommodation," maintaining that in the United States, "institutions presuppose a Supreme Being and that the government's accepting of God does not constitute the formation of a state church which the Founding Fathers prohibited in the Constitution."[63]

What did the Founding Fathers say about religion, morals, and ethics?

"Religion is the only solid basis of good morals; therefore, education should teach the precepts of religion and the duties of man towards God." (Gouverneur Morris signed the Articles of Confederation and wrote the preamble to the United States Constitution.[64])

"Of all the dispositions and habits which lead to political prosperity, religion and morality are the indispensable supports…In vain would that man claim the tribute of patriotism who should labor to subvert these great pillars of human happiness, these firmest props of the duties of men and citizens." (President George Washington[65])

"Statesmen, my dear Sir, may plan and speculate for liberty, but it is Religion and Morality alone, which can establish the Principles upon which Freedom can securely stand." (John Adams, Second President[66])

"And let us with caution indulge the supposition that morality can be maintained without religion…reason and experience both forbid us to expect that national morality can prevail in exclusion of religious principle." (President George Washington[67])

"To preserve the government, we must also preserve morals. Morality rests on religion, if you destroy the foundation, the superstructure must fall. When the public mind becomes vitiated and corrupt, laws are a nullity, and constitutions are but wastepaper."[68] (Daniel Webster was in the U.S. House of Representatives and U.S. Senate and was a U.S. Secretary of State.)

"The moral principles contained in the Scriptures ought to form the basis of all our civil constitutions and laws...All the miseries and evils which men suffer from vice, crime, ambition, injustice, oppression, slavery and war, proceed from their despising or neglecting the precepts contained in the Bible."[69] (Noah Webster wrote the first "Compendious Dictionary of the English Language" in 1806 and was in the Connecticut House of Representatives. He has been called "The Father of American Scholarship and Education." He was in the Connecticut Militia during the Revolutionary War and elected a Fellow of the American Academy of Arts and Sciences in 1799.)

So, what has happened to our morals and ethics? Are Americans exhibiting more harmful behaviors because of copying the habits they see on TV shows, media productions, video games, and violent movies, maybe just copying classmates or parents, or is it believing that whatever the Internet tells them is universal truth? Does the news media have any influence when they keep showing and hyping negative news again and again? Is it because people spend so much time focusing and relying on their phones for short bits of incomplete information instead of reading in-depth magazine/newspaper articles or books?

What was on the minds of people 18-30 or older during the Pandemic that they seemed to be indifferent toward passing any virus to their parents, grandparents, or others? Is it the result of their overconsuming alcohol or drugs, or is it the Internet's anything-goes propaganda that was deadening their heartfelt emotions and their feelings for others?

Our personal addictive behaviors are amplified by our daily acceptance of Internet platforms as essential to maintaining our social and cultural interaction. It does not matter how negative, untruthful, deceptive, immoral, or anti-religious they are; all these avenues we input into our consciousness influence how we think and feel about ourselves and others.

People today can become super rich, have large mansions, and live lifestyles where they are always plugged into their electronic devices, feeling they can have whatever they want whenever they want it. But unless people have a positive moral and ethical foundation of personal beliefs, their desires for instant satisfaction and flamboyant lifestyles can easily develop into a continuum of addictive behaviors. If this is what people want to help formulate and manifest within their personal identity, they may find many rude awakenings along their life's journey.

US VERSUS THEM

In the United States, we now live in a society that is a combination of an "aristocracy," a "meritocracy," and a "representative democracy." What do these terms mean?

ARISTOCRACY - While ancient Greeks classified an aristocracy as ruled by the best moral and intellectually superior citizens who ruled in the interest of everyone, aristocracy has developed to mean rule by the privileged upper layer of a stratified group. Today, that privileged economic/political group is generally defined as those with the most money who can run for office and pay for an expensive campaign with the help of friends, corporate donations, and political action committees.

MERITOCRACY – This is a rule or control by a group with the greatest competency and ability to create wealth. Moral or ethical behavior may not be necessary, but the ability to produce wealth is probably the most important aspect of their personal, political, and corporate lives.

REPRESENTATIVE DEMOCRACY – This is an indirect democracy where eligible voters elect representatives who make the laws and regulations for everyone on their behalf. These elected officials are not legally bound to vote the way the public who elected them wants them to vote. A Representative government can be inefficient with large, slow bureaucracies that can be corrupt when those who are elected seek monetary or political gain for themselves instead of serving those who elected them.

It is easy to see why our country has so many injustices. The rich and super-rich are the governing and industrial leaders, with corporate and technological industries having the greatest ability to directly influence lawmakers through political donations, lobbyists, and the offers of corporate jobs after political terms end.

Today, there seem to be very few Presidents or legislators like Lincoln or Washington in the higher echelons of political power, though some may exist at lower levels of state and local governments.

How did politics get so weird and vengeful in the United States?

The social, ethical, moral, and political ideals that many of Our Founding Fathers professed prior to the writing of the Declaration of Independence changed prior to the formulation and writing of the United States Constitution.

The Scottish and French Enlightenment Eras that developed for decades leading up to the American Revolution had focused on the rights of individuals in society, with inalienable rights endowed by their Creator. After the American Revolution, Benjamin Franklin and Thomas Jefferson shipped off to Europe for years to represent the new "freed from England, colonial states." These men were classically educated in Greek and Roman history, literature, cultural thinking, and statesmanship.

While these scholars were gone, new American coalitions with alternative political and economic perspectives for the country were forming in the states. When Jefferson returned from France and saw what had changed, he started abandoning some of the classical ideologies that he had used to write the Declaration of Independence. These new political and ideological perspectives drew his attention.

With the Revolutionary War now over, various wealthy individuals in positions of power and business that were once aligned with the British, were now assuming legislative positions in major cities like New York, Philadelphia, and other communities. These new politicians professed that our nation's original Federalist leaders were not only "out of step" with current ideas but also that those current old ideas would never work with a new form of factional party politics. These new parties said that the Federalists were so lost in the past that they might as well be classified as enemies of the newly formed and modernized political party system.

These contemporary and wealthy politicians and legislators disregarded the classical ideals of virtue and morality, finding them no longer significant or important in political governing. Older Enlightenment Era politicians felt that these new factional-based parties were using a "group think" propaganda approach to gather new converts. These new factional legislators felt that only a political party of like-minded members would produce true solutions for successful governing.

James Madison, a close confidant of Jefferson's, who would eventually become the Fourth President, had now aligned himself with the idea that political parties were the solution to getting things done in governmental affairs. He and Jefferson started a newspaper called the "National Gazette," which Jefferson heavily financed, in which they both wrote articles pseudonymously. Their main platform spoke against the Federalist ideas of how the country should be politically governed. A college friend of Madison's, who was a paid employee of the U.S. Secretary of State's Office, edited the paper, and Jefferson also participated in this activity. At the same time, he was still Secretary of State in the Federalist Cabinet. He was conspiring against President Washington who had hired him.

The National Gazette strongly criticized Washington and his policies. A high degree of mudslinging was common practice at the Gazette. Today, these types of activities might be compared to a publication, which might be a combination of OAN, The National Inquirer, Breitbart News Network, and FOX NEWS.

Madison wrote that the solutions to factional-based political problems in government could only be achieved through rivalry, partisanship politics, contention, and competition, which he thought would naturally result in compromises. We have seen from 2008 to the current timeframe, where ego-based political party shenanigans have led the country into times of mass chaos, hateful speech, and prejudice against all levels of political leadership. This has culminated in a new political focus of "I'm right and not only are my foes wrong, but they are evil." This new negative political rhetoric has been preached by both our country's leaders and its citizens.

The result of a political party's inflexibility and unwillingness to compromise has led to a dysfunctional way of governing. Covid-19 is an excellent example. The death of over 1,000,000 American citizens has still not convinced many politicians to abandon their biases against science.

Alexander Hamilton had warned the citizenry that claims by political factions could turn masses of the public into deluded and fanatical followers who were being seduced by political lies and deceptions. Maybe Hamilton unknowingly foresaw the effects of QANON and deep-seeded negative political party propaganda that preached the 2020 Presidential Election was rigged against their faction, even after every state election verification, every vote recount, and all courts ruled against that premise.

When Washington finished his second term as President, he warned the American people that they should never forget the importance of a cohesive National Union that is based not on adherence to a political party's ideologies and propaganda but on the value and virtue of the individual citizen who sought unity and harmony among their leaders.

John Adams followed Washington as President, and his administration encountered opposing outcries for political party populism. Adams had led a more common man lifestyle near Boston, where he grew up on his father's 9.5-acre farm in Braintree, Massachusetts, about 15 miles south of Boston. His father came from a lineage of Puritans and was a farmer, a minister, and a shoemaker. Adams did not have the golden lifestyle opportunities that Jefferson had in aristocratic Virginia, where Jefferson owned 5000 Acres of plantations worked by Negro slaves.

Adams went from living on his father's small farm to a rented "clapboard" house in Boston. After several other home moves in Boston, Adams, his wife, and children moved back to the family farm after his father died in 1774, two years before the Declaration of Independence. Of the first 12 United States Presidents, only Adams and John Q. Adams did not own any slaves. What does this say about the morals and ethics followed by the leaders of these new political factions after Adams left office?

Two thousand years ago, the great Greek philosopher Plutarch told citizens that they should seek out and support politicians that are honest instead of popular. He also wrote that politicians should not excessively praise themselves but should conduct themselves while in politics with a positive moral philosophy toward all whom they govern. Are we seeing these approaches practiced in America today?

THEN VERSUS NOW

The greater the personal use of technology in your life, the more control the aristocrats and meritocratic technocrats have over you. They control almost all the audio and visual inputs you are receiving through the Internet, TV, advertising, and the products available for you to purchase.

These same industrial and technological leaders provide you with the substances that feed most of your addictive behaviors as they supply you with questionable foods, drugs, alcohol, porn, and whatever products you purchase and use. Through advertising techniques, they enhance products to make them seem bigger and better than you might have imagined them to be before you saw the product being over-advertised. This advertising takes place 24/7 on most TV channels, radio stations, and Internet sites.

Somewhere in your consciousness, people might recognize what these companies are doing, but that does not seem to stop many people from making poor choices. This attitude is not surprising. People mimic the behaviors they see on television, in movies, on the Internet, among their friends, or the activities or words spoken by some of our political leaders.

We know that large corporations do massive research on how to influence people concerning their buying habits. Their product advertising methods are created to attract your attention and your addictive behavioral inclinations. Companies know an amazing amount of information about you by tracking all your Internet searches and behaviors on social media sites. Every keystroke, every item you click on to seek more information about any subject, every search you make, and everything you buy using a credit or debit card are all recorded. Companies know where you live, how you spend your money, and when and where you travel. When you accept their Terms of Use, you permit them to track almost everything about you. Almost all your public records can be easily accessed.

Let's just call it a given that all these companies have many highly educated specialists in dozens of fields of study that work on methods to influence your mind and your choices. They do so by giving you the right advertising input with their professional advice to persuade and convince you what you should buy or believe. These companies pay their business advisors and marketers huge sums of money to create the influences that cause you to accept, act, and purchase what they want you to buy or the propaganda their businesses want you to believe is true.

But what about the advice and philosophies given to you by our politicians? After all, these people are those that we, ourselves, elect to guide us through all aspects of government, including creating the laws that citizens should follow. Governmental rulings, thousands of regulations and standards, and political influences reach deep into your life in hundreds of ways. How qualified are these lawmakers to decide what is right for each citizen in the country?

American politicians do not need to have any college degrees or personal experiences in medical, economic, agricultural, geopolitical, environmental, educational, or scientific matters to create laws and regulations, or understand how these laws may negatively affect the lives of all the citizens of the United States. Many of the decisions they make in creating the laws and regulations they enact are heavily guided by the political contributions they receive from donors and friends. So, what are the job experiences of our legislators that qualify them for their jobs?

The House of Representatives in the 117th Congress had 173 members with law degrees, while the Senate had 57. The House had 273 Congressmen with business backgrounds, and the Senate had 47. There were 14 physicians in the House and 4 in the Senate.[70] Here are some of the business careers and backgrounds of the lawmakers in the House and Senate: software company executives, management consultants, bankers, real estate executives, automobile dealers, and venture capitalists.

With a majority of both the House and Senate members being lawyers and business executives, is it no wonder that our leaders had a hard time comprehending the extent and seriousness of a Pandemic? The COVID-19 outbreak in 2020 occurred when many of our rulers gave our citizens advice that was the opposite of what our highly trained and skilled medical community was trying to tell the public. (If you want to know what was happening behind the scenes concerning the COVID-19 pandemic, read the book "Premonition" by Michael Lewis.) The lies and misjudgments of our politicians showed you what can happen when our leaders are lawyers and business professionals who think they know more about the health and welfare of our citizens than our medical professionals. Lawyers defend people and corporations in court, and business professionals focus on building wealth and corporate prosperity, especially for those in the top 10% of wealth who own about 90% of all the country's assets. Corporate laws and tax policies are written first to benefit the wealthy, with the rest of the country's workforce waiting for when that promised trickle-down prosperity reaches them. Our country's income inequality has been growing for over 40 years. This is what occurs when many of our lawmakers are in the pockets of corporations.

There is another aspect of life in the United States that needs to be addressed and that is DEBT. I came across an interesting website. It is the United States Debt Clock, which can be reached online at USDebt-Clock.org. You may be amazed at what you can learn if you check this web location. Its main feature is the continual running figures for how much the Federal National Debt is increasing by the second. There is more information on the page: the growing student loan debt, American's credit card debt, our country's debt held by foreign countries, the U.S. trade deficit, U.S. interest paid, family savings, Federal spending, state and local debt, and dozens of other tallies of who owes what and where the money is going. Do our leaders tell you about these statistics?

Why does the United States Congress, along with recent Presidents and their Cabinets, most bureaucracies, and the corporate/business world keep telling you that going into debt forever is how a country succeeds? President Eisenhower did not believe this while he was in office, and even with high tax rates back then, the country did well.

If the Federal Government does not care about having a balanced budget, why should average families care? The reason that families should care is that, unlike the Federal Government, families cannot print "money from nothing." Every year, politicians increase the debt level because they want to spend more on tax breaks for the rich, forever increasing non-audited wasteful military spending and funding thousands of pet projects for their districts or business friends back home. Pet projects are used to convince the people back home that their representatives care about the people in their district. But are many of these pet projects, like the famous "bridge to nowhere project," justified expenditures?

People who seriously study economics have stated for many decades that you need to increase debt during hard times, but in good times, you pay down the debt because the economy is doing well or booming. That is not the reality of what our politicians have been doing for a long time. They increase the debt by borrowing huge amounts in both bad times and good times – totally illogical economics with no common sense at all.

Look around you. Is your continual debt accumulation making you a healthier, wealthier, and happier person?

While Ronald Reagan was President, he issued Executive Order 12369 on June 30, 1982, for a commission to come up with solutions on how "to drain the swamp" of unnecessary government spending. The Commission was headed by J. Peter Grace and composed of business experts who were privately funded by donations. The official name was "The Private Sector Survey on Cost Control" (PSSCC). The final report was published about 18 months later.[71]

It reported that if certain recommendations were put into place, there would be 424-billion-dollar savings in three years, and by the year 2000 the savings could be almost 2 trillion dollars. Reagan basically ignored the report, and over the coming years, very few recommendations became reality. The U.S. National Debt rose to 13 trillion dollars in 2010, and now, fourteen years later, according to the US Debt Clock, it is around 34.71 trillion (on May 5, 2024), which turns out to be about $267,000 per taxpayer. But the United States' Total Debt is over $99.98 trillion.

Why are these Debt Clock figures and calculations so important? They show how, instead of having both balanced government and family budgets, our addictive overspending overrides our innate common sense. All this debt creates heavy drags on our country's and our family's economic futures. American citizens' personal credit card debt is currently near 1.4 trillion dollars, about $8,340 per holder. Student loan debt $39,000 each.

The Federal Reserve publishes vast amounts of statistical information on the status of debt in the United States. I recently came across one of their publications, "History of the Public Debt," for Fiscal Year 2020, which ended in September 2020. This information covered the United States Public Government Debt over the last 20 years. I then compared this with the changes in population during the same 20-year period. This is the result of what happened during those 20 years: our population increased by about 18%, and our National Debt went up by about 476%. Considering that the U.S. Congress creates the legislation that produces the spending programs, and the President signs the legislation into law, do you think that these two branches of our government are doing a very good job managing the country's finances?

Overspending is one potential side effect of people's addictive behaviors toward consumption, but almost everyone is doing it, so why stop? Why follow our government's example? Buying to satisfy "needs" can help create lasting family harmony and prosperity. Buying to satisfy "wants" traps you into more addictive spending.

Thomas Jefferson once said: "to preserve our independence, we must not let our rulers load us with perpetual debt." In America, voters for most of the last 60 years have elected Presidents and Legislators who do not have fiscally sound public debt policies. To get elected and stay elected, they make sugar-coated promises about how they are going to look out for the people's welfare. These unrealistic fantasies are like using little bandages for a hemorrhaging cut desperately needing surgery.

It is not the unqualified President's or Legislators' fault. It is the voter's fault for choosing the wrong people for the jobs. Instead of electing the most popular candidates, voters should be choosing the most qualified people. Greek philosophers have been telling us this for over 2000 years. The Founding Fathers knew and understood what the Greeks were saying because they repeated it prior to the American Revolution.

Wake up, Americans! Rich professional politicians and businessmen are not going to bail you out of your personal debt or the national debt. They will promise you sweet remedies, but they will administer you bitter pills, claiming that you should peacefully suffer in silence. While they retire in luxury, you, your children, and your grandchildren pay now and in the future for politicians' inactions in dealing with this important debt issue.

With the top ten percent of wealthy individuals controlling the political and economic structure of the United States, some of the latest 2024 surveys show that 53% of American families can't afford to pay a $1000 emergency expense. A want more, buy more, go into debt more attitude is crippling the family structure and livelihood. Instead of listening to our innate common sense, we follow the advice of advertising propaganda that never stops being sent to us from every technological device we own.

If you were alive or read about the indoctrination that occurred in Germany prior to World War II, that continued prior to, during, and continuing after the Korean War, and what has occurred in Russia for the last 80 or more years, you would realize that the techniques modern technology is using to influence your minds today used to be called brainwashing back then. History says this type of activity does not turn out well for any society.

Chapter 10

RECENT PAST PRESIDENTS

What makes a good leader for a country? I have mentioned several qualities and philosophies that Our Founding Fathers proposed in formulating our country and have shown the types of leadership qualities our early 1787-1808 pioneers displayed in expanding from the original colonies into the Ohio frontier. What about the more current qualities of America's Presidential leadership during the last 60-70 years?

A liberal like John F. Kennedy, with his Camelot persona and a wealthy New England lifestyle, tried to set forth a future-focused agenda when he was elected. Though an ex-WWII military officer, his upbringing came from an aristocratic family. He spoke of a bold new frontier, with an increased exploration of outer space and promises of Americans setting foot on the moon. "Space, the final frontier," as the TV show "Star Trek" announced at the start of each episode. Though he loved to mingle and connect with the populace, showing his big grin, his elite background limited his understanding of the struggles within the lower classes. Old-world biases had a hard time accepting his bright outlook with new-world perspectives. He wanted to be seen in the public arena and, as such, seemed to have a naivete of protecting himself from those who did not favor his projected big social and governmental changes.

He and his wife presented a wealthy, picture-perfect aura, lifestyle, and marriage, but that lifestyle was held by few Americans and envied by others. His Camelot image warmed the hearts of many citizens who perceived him more like a benevolent king. Still, this image conflicted with the multitudes of poor and disadvantaged people of color who had few opportunities for good jobs and medical assistance. They could dream about his Camelot hopes, but it was just another fantasy when they woke up every morning without sufficient food for their children.

Kennedy's after-death image was tarnished when it was discovered that his affairs with other women were kept hidden by the Secret Service. Some of his Rat Pack movie star friends might have led him astray with their Hollywood lifestyle behaviors. As a result, his glowing, untarnished public image did not reflect the reality of his marital infidelity.

During his inaugural address after getting elected, Kennedy made a statement that people still remember 60 years later: "Ask not what your country can do for you – ask what you can do for your country."[72]

Kennedy had to deal with the Cuban Missile Crisis, which almost brought the United States to nuclear war. I remember the Duck and Cover drills in grade school during this time frame. He also started the Peace Corps, dealt with the Berlin Crisis, and signed the Nuclear Test Ban Treaty with Russia in 1963. Kennedy was assassinated on November 22, 1963, and there has always been a tremendous amount of controversy about his killing pertaining to Lee Harvey Oswald, Jack Ruby, the Mafia, and the Warren Commission.

Lyndon B. Johnson, who became President with the Kennedy Assassination, was perceived by his friends and family as a quiet, retired, "ranching grandfather" who was more familiar with the problems of poverty, disparity, and inequality. But in public and behind the scenes of politics, "he was a man who relished power, a master manipulator, who harnessed his finely tuned political instincts to achieve lofty goals."[73]Johnson felt he needed to do something to help the many disadvantaged people in the country. He had grown up amid hardship working on neighboring farms, being a shoe-shine boy, and he trapped and sold animal skins. During

1928-1929, he was a teacher at a mainly Mexican American school in Cotulla, Texas. He also served as the Director of the National Youth Administration in Texas, a U.S. House Representative, and a U.S. Senator before being picked as Kennedy's Vice President.

Once he became President, he addressed the War on Poverty with the Office of Economic Opportunity, which consisted of the Job Corps, Volunteers in Service to America (VISTA), the Work-Study Program, the Work Experience Program, and the Community Action Program, which administered Head Start.

Then there was the Civil Rights Act, the Voting Rights Act, Medicare and Medicaid, the Clean Water Restoration Act, and the Clean Air Act for automobiles.

But there was also Vietnam, where in 1968, our troop numbers reached 550,000. We eventually abandoned the people of South Vietnam after losses of 58,000 American troops and 300,000 wounded. North Vietnam lost about a million troops, and the combined civilian losses for both North and South Vietnam were about 2,000,000. In the end, North Vietnam took over South Vietnam, and it is now just Vietnam.

In his early childhood, Richard Nixon also grew up in poverty, and he almost died a couple of times of injuries and pneumonia before he was five. He graduated first in his class in high school and received two awards for academic excellence. In college, he played football and, as a senior, was class president before graduating second in his class and receiving a scholarship to Duke University Law School. He served in the Navy for about four years, finishing as a lieutenant commander.[74]

Nixon had plenty of previous international experience as Vice President of the United States from 1953-1961. As President, he started winding down the number of American forces in South Vietnam. In 1970, he invaded Cambodia with 70,000 troops, but the venture failed to achieve its objective. Eventually, all American forces were withdrawn from Vietnam after massive student and citizen protests across our country.

Some of Nixon's accomplishments were: The Chemical Weapons Treaty of 1971, the SALT agreement with Russia limiting antiballistic missile sites, Wage-Price Controls 1971-3, establishing the Environmental Protection Agency, the Consumer Product Safety Act, landing a man on the moon, and the ratifying of the Twenty-sixth Amendment to the Constitution which lowered the voting age from 21 to 18.

Then came the Watergate problem, which was his illegal attempt to try to ensure that he would get reelected to a second term as President. In the process, many people in his administration were arrested, went to jail, paid a fine, or were disgraced. In the end, Nixon was viewed as a lying crook, and the Watergate incident forced him to resign instead of being impeached and removed from office.

Gerald Ford was the next President. He grew up in central Michigan in modest circumstances and, at around 12, learned that he was adopted. He did well academically in high school, was a star athlete on the football team, and had a part-time job frying burgers at a restaurant. During his senior year in college, he was voted "most valuable player and played in the 1935 College All-Star game against the Chicago Bears. Both the Detroit Lions and Green Bay Packers offered him a professional contract, but he turned them down to study law."[75]

He served in the Navy from 1942-46, finishing as a lieutenant commander. He was elected to the U.S. House of Representatives and was a House Minority Leader 1965-73 and Vice President 1973-4.

Ford was the only President who was never elected President or Vice President. Besides pardoning President Nixon, he signed the Helsinki Agreement, signed four Consumerism Bills, converted the Atomic Energy Commission to the Nuclear Regulatory Commission, and signed the Campaign Reform Law of 1974. He also faced two assassination attempts by women. He was a decent man and a loving husband throughout his political career, something the country really needed after Nixon.

Jimmy Carter was a born-again Christian peanut farmer from Georgia. It is said that he was the first president born in a hospital. The home where he spent his childhood did not have running water or electricity. People probably do not know that Carter was a speed reader capable of reading

2000 words a minute with 95% comprehension. He graduated from the United States Naval Academy in Annapolis and served from 1946-1953. In 1951, he joined the nuclear submarine program, studied nuclear physics at Union College, and was an engineering officer aboard the Sea Wolf, one of the earliest nuclear submarines. In 1953, he resigned from the Navy to manage the family farm after his father died.

After being a Georgia State Senator, he was elected Governor of Georgia. In his acceptance speech after being nominated by the Democratic party for the Presidency on July 15, 1976, he said: "It is time to honor and strengthen our families and our neighborhoods and our diverse cultures and customs." With Carter being elected President, he was the first Deep South person elected since Zachary Taylor in 1848.

Being a successful President was tough for him during stagflation, the Arab Oil Crisis, the Iranian Revolution, and the Iranian Hostage Crisis, but the Camp David Israel and Egypt Peace Treaty was an important accomplishment.

Today, he is more highly regarded as conscientious and hard-working for Habitat for Humanity and other projects that have benefited tens of thousands of citizens. During three years of his Presidency, the nation's economy grew at 5% each year, a figure that is more than double what has been occurring during the last decade.

Ronald Reagan was a former Republican Hollywood movie and TV actor. He was born in the family's five-room rented apartment above a bakery in Tampico, Illinois, weighing 10 pounds. Early teen jobs involved him digging house foundations and being a roustabout for 25 cents per hour when the Ringling Brothers Circus passed through town. He played football in both high school and college and was also a student body president in each school. After college, he went into radio broadcasting as a weekend sportscaster in Davenport, Iowa.

He married the actress Jane Wyman and was the first president to be divorced. He later married Nancy Davis, also a Hollywood actor. They acted together in a movie called "Hellcats of the Navy" in 1957. Reagan acted from 1937-1965. You might remember him as the host of the TV show "Death Valley Days." The next step in his career was as Governor of California. Here, I remember a slight connection to Reagan. In the summer of 1969, I rented a room at a college fraternity house in Sacramento, California. The fraternity rented rooms when the school was not in regular school sessions. I was taking a college night class and working a day job as a migrant farm worker for $1.65 an hour. Five other guys were also renting summer rooms at the fraternity house, and they were all political interns at the California State Capitol building. Every night, they filled me in on the unusual activities and corporate connections of Governor Reagan. It was a real eye-opener.

Reagan defeated Jimmy Carter in the Electoral College in a landslide, 489 to 49. Reagan then won a second term, beating Mondale by a vote of 525 to 13, the largest electoral vote difference in American history.

Reagan was famous for "Reaganomics" (supply-side economics) – the combination of tax cuts and big increases in defense spending. During his Presidency, Conservatives started a culture war against traditional liberals, divorce, sexual freedom, abortion, and homosexuality.[76]

Reagan was wounded in an assassination attempt, which brought him even more popularity among voters. Reagan's Immigration Reform and Control Act granted amnesty to 3 million illegal immigrants. He and his wife instituted the War on Drugs with the slogan "Just Say No." Reagan was known for the Voting Rights Act, the Iran Contra Scandal, and the end of the Cold War.

George H.W. Bush grew up in a rich suburb of New York City, living in a nine-bedroom mansion, and often spent summers as a child at his maternal grandfather's stone house on 11 acres in Kennebunkport, Maine. At 13, following other wealthy families' children, he attended an exclusive prep school in Andover, Massachusetts, where in his senior year, he became president of the class, captain of the baseball and soccer teams, and editor of the school paper. While attending Yale University, he played in the 1947 and 1948 NCAA College Baseball World Series.

Prior to attending Yale, Bush enlisted in the Navy on his 18th birthday, June 12, 1942, where he served until September 1945. He became the youngest pilot in the Navy at that time. Bush flew 58 combat missions in a three-man, single-engine Grumman Avenger torpedo bomber, logging 1,228 flight hours. Once his plane was shot down by antiaircraft fire, and his other two airmen died during the incident.

After the war, he got into the oil business, and after much success, he got into politics as a conservative Republican speaking against the Nuclear Test Ban Treaty and Civil Rights Act but lost in his first election attempt. He eventually won two U.S. House of Representatives elections as a moderate Republican. President Nixon appointed him to be U.S. Ambassador to the United Nations, and then in 1973, he took the job as Chairman of the Republican National Committee during the Watergate scandal.

President Ford appointed him Director of the Central Intelligence Agency, and later, he became Vice President under Ronald Reagan, where, during the Iran Contra Scandal, he played a shady role but was never directly implicated. In the 1988 Presidential race, he handily beat Michael Dukakis with an electoral margin of 426 to 111.

As President, he led a successful Operation Desert Shield that kicked Saddam Hussein out of Kuwait. It was discovered that 15% of U.S. casualties died from U.S. forces friendly fire. Bush spearheaded the North Atlantic Free Trade Agreement (NAFTA) between the United States, Canada, and Mexico, which allowed manufacturers to shut down factories in the U.S. and move them to Mexico. Under Bush, budget deficits continued to grow. The Savings and Loan Crisis showed how rich people could mismanage mortgages and money ventures that created huge financial problems for banks, the poor, and the middle-class, while these same people walked away from the crisis still rich.

Bush heavily campaigned with the theme, "No New Taxes," then, in disbelief of the populace, raised taxes when in office. He also pardoned all the political Republican higher-ups connected to Reagan's Iran Contra Scandal. Later, third-party candidate H. Ross Perot entered the Presidential race, and in the next election, Bush lost to Clinton.

William Jefferson Clinton grew up in Hope, Arkansas in a modest home. His stepfather's alcoholism created problems for him and his abused mother during his childhood, where he often had to step in between his parents. Clinton became a member of the Boy Scouts and led a typical baby-boomer childhood and, at one point, won first place in a state saxophone competition. He formed a sunglass-wearing, three-man band called the Three Blind Mice.

As a member of an Arkansas American Legion program called Boys' Nation, he attended an outdoor gathering at the White House in Washington, D.C., where he had an opportunity to shake President Kennedy's hand. In high school, he was a member of the National Honor Society and a semi-finalist in the National Merit Scholarship contest. He attended Georgetown University where he was president of the freshman and sophomore classes. He went to England as a Rhodes scholar at Oxford University where he demonstrated his anti-Vietnam War stance.

Instead of finishing his third year of the Rhodes scholarship, in 1970 he left England and received a scholarship to Yale University Law School. He supported and worked for anti-war Democrats.

In October 1975, he married Hillary Rodham, whose father owned a textile company. She was raised in Park Ridge, an affluent northwest suburb of Chicago. She was a conservative Republican who supported Barry Goldwater for President when she was a senior in high school. But once becoming a student at Wellesley College, she turned into a Vietnam War protester. Hillary met Clinton while both attended Yale Law School.

Bill Clinton was a law professor at the University of Arkansas, Attorney General of Arkansas, and finally Governor of Arkansas. As a candidate for the Presidency, Clinton won only 43% of the national vote because H. Ross Perot got 19%, but Clinton won the Electoral College 370 to 168.

Clinton got the name "Slick Willie" attached to him by other politicians. While in office, he got passed both tax increases and budget cuts, and this, combined with a strong economy, led to the first budget surplus since the 1960s. In one of the biggest blunders of his Presidency, he signed the Gramm-Leach-Bliley Act, which repealed part of the Glass-Steagall Act of 1933. Clinton wanted the financial services industry, which consisted of big political financial contributors, to be less regulated. The result of that repeal eventually caused the Great Recession of 2007-8. He also signed a regulation that would loosen other controls on Commodity

Trading which resulted in the Enron collapse and rip-off. Clinton signed a bill giving China "most favored nation status," and we now see the result of that decision.

Though married to Hillary, other women rumored about romances and sexual experiences. Then, as President, after his affair with Monica, Clinton was charged with two counts of impeachment in the U.S. House of Representatives, but the Senate voted against impeachment. It seems that only Clinton could define one word in his special kind of way.

"It depends on what the meaning of the word "is," is. If the-if he- if 'is' means is and never has been, that is not – that is one thing. If it means there is none, that was a completely true statement…Now if someone had asked me on that day, are you having any kind of sexual relations with Ms. Lewinsky, that is, asked me a question in the present tense, I would have said no. And it would have been completely true."[77]

George W. Bush was the son of former President George H. W. Bush. George W. attended the same exclusive prep high school in Massachusetts as his father. Then, following in his father's and grandfather's footsteps, he attended and graduated from Yale, where history became his major field of study. Unlike his father, he was only an average student and was not a standout in sports. Instead of letting his student draft deferment lapse, he enrolled in training to become a pilot in the Texas Air National Guard. There was controversy about not fulfilling his commitment to the Guard, but he was discharged from the Guard and entered Harvard Business School. After completing that curriculum, he returned to Midland, Texas, worked as an oil and gas attorney, and later started his own business in that field. After a talk with the Reverend Billy Graham, a family friend, he quit drinking alcohol. Bush, after several lucrative business transactions, went on to become the Governor of Texas. As Governor, he favored punishment by death for certain crimes people committed. He served four terms as Governor. While later running for the U.S. Presidency, there was controversy about his previous use of illegal drugs, which he said he had quit in 1974. Bush was one of four people running for President, and the election was so close that it was a decision by the U.S. Supreme Court to stop a Florida statewide recount of an extremely close vote count there that gave him the Florida victory and the resulting U.S. Presidency. Bush won the Electoral College vote count by 271 to 266. You needed 270 to be declared the winner.

The Bush administration decided that it was not going to abide by the Kyoto Protocol reducing the emissions of gases into the atmosphere and it withdrew from the 1972 Anti-Ballistic Missile Treaty. The events of the 9/11 Terrorist Attack happened during his Presidency. He placed a heavy focus on Surveillance and Homeland Security in America saying that our country had to defeat and eliminate terrorism. Anyone who saw the pictures of the prisoners who were inhumanely treated at the Abu Ghraib prison in Iraq might think that some of our behaviors seemed to suggest we, too, acted like terrorists to those we did not like.

In June 2006, the U.S. Supreme Court ruled that the potential procedures the U.S. Government was going to use on Guantanamo prisoners charged with war crimes was a violation of the Geneva Conventions and the Uniform Code of Military Justice.

Under Bush's directive, the world was told through speeches in the United Nations Assembly that Saddam Hussein manufactured and stored massive quantities of Weapons of Mass Destruction that Hussein could use against the United States and the rest of the world. Our U.N. delegation told the world that Hussein must be stopped and his ability to use these weapons of destruction must end. As a result, mostly United States troops, with help from a coalition of other countries, invaded Iraq.

In the end, no Weapons of Mass Destruction were found. While Bush was President, the early phases of the Afghanistan War (2001 to end in 2021) were conducted, the War in Iraq was started and sort of ended, and the Recession of 2007-8 took place. The Afghan War cost 2400 American soldier deaths, with 20,000 wounded. 145,000 Afghan troops and civilians were killed, and that war cost at least $1 billion. The Iraq War had 7,000 Americans killed and 53,000 wounded; Iraqi deaths were about 460,000 and cost $1-1.5 trillion dollars.[78] [79]

When Bush first took office, his approval ratings were about 50%, then they went to 92% after 9/11, then collapsed to 19% after leaving office, a record low for any President of the United States.[80][81] In retirement, Bush became more introspective with a positive, artistic outlook.

Barack Obama was the first African American President of the United States. Obama's schooling went from Punahou School, a private elite school in Hawaii, to Occidental College in Los Angeles, to Columbia University in New York City, to graduating magna cum laude from Harvard Law School in 1991. He moved to Chicago and worked with low-income residents in black communities and public housing on the South Side of the city. His future wife, Michelle, was also a graduate of Harvard Law School, and they met while Obama was working as a summer associate at a Chicago law firm.

In 1996, he won election to the Illinois Senate representing the South Side of Chicago. As Senator, he opposed the War in Iraq and, speaking at an outdoor rally in Chicago in October 2002 against the war, said: "I am not opposed to all wars. I am opposed to dumb wars…a successful war against Iraq will require a U.S. occupation of undetermined length, at undetermined cost, with undetermined consequences."

After being elected and only serving one term as a U.S. Senator, he decided to run for President, which he won and was inaugurated on January 20, 2009. The Republicans in Congress fought him "tooth and nail" about every form of legislation he tried to get passed. His biggest success was getting the Affordable Care Act (Obamacare) passed. He put forth the American Recovery Act, which helped bail out many areas of the economy after the Great Recession. During his administration, he signed the Paris Agreement on Climate Change, had our troops kill Osama bin Laden, got the "Don't Ask, Don't Tell" Act repealed, and signed the Dodd-Frank Wall Street Reform and Consumer Protection Act. The Unemployment Rate went from 10% to 4.7% during his two terms as President. In 2012, he deported 400,000 illegal immigrants. Drone deployment was a major focus of his to combat terrorists and any of our foreign enemies. After withdrawing many U.S. forces from Iraq, ISIS fighting forces substantially increased in number, and they vastly increased the areas of Iraq they controlled.

Obama's birthplace, race, and name drew a lot of attention and finger-pointing from Republicans and a future President. Obama also seemed to "draw a line in the sand" against the President of Syria, but he did not seem to follow through when the Syrian President crossed that line with increased poison gas attacks against his own Syrian people. Obama had to deal with many beratements from Republicans, especially in one State of the Union Address when a Republican Congressman called Obama a "liar" while Obama was addressing the nation and assembly.

While Obama was President, the U.S. Supreme Court legalized gay marriage in June 2015. Obama's administration organized the Iran Nuclear Deal, allowing outside inspectors to examine Iran's nuclear program of enriching uranium in return for lifting some sanctions against Iran.

According to Gallup, Obama's approval rating at the start of his Presidency was 82%. By December 2009, it fell to 51%, then 40% in August 2011, and he finished the Presidency at 57%.[82]

I would like to discuss another President who was a better overall leader than those I have previously mentioned. Dwight D. Eisenhower was born in 1890 to David and Ida. Both parents were disciplinarians, and "family life revolved around work and Bible study." [83] Though the family belonged to the Mennonite River Brethren community and Dwight read from the Bible at family gatherings, after leaving home for the Army, he did not attend any churches until 1953 when he was baptized at National Presbyterian Church in Washington D.C.[84] Dwight shared the house chores, worked in the garden, and took care of the animals. He also sold his vegetables in town from a cart he dragged around.

Later in life, Dwight remembered fishing, hunting, and camping as a youth. "The life we had together," he wrote, "had been complete, stimulating, and informative, with opportunity available to us for the asking. We had been poor, but one of the glories of America, at the time, was that we didn't know it. It was a good, secure, small-town life, and that we wanted for luxuries didn't occur to any of us."[85]

Dwight enrolled in West Point in June 1911 at 20 years old. World War I ended before he had an opportunity to serve in Europe. In 1920, he and

Mamie, his wife, were met with the death of their three-year-old son from scarlet fever. Dwight kept rising in the army ranks under Generals Pershing and MacArthur in the 1920s and 1930s. In 1939, Dwight was a 49-year-old lieutenant colonel stationed in the Philippines. Still, in less than three years, he was a General controlling the entire European Theater of Operations that defeated Hitler and other Axis powers.[86]

After the War, Eisenhower gave a speech at Guildhall in London that demonstrated Eisenhower's touch of "gracious humility, plain spoken earnestness, and a willingness to give credit to others."[87]

"At this moment of triumph, Eisenhower was 55 years old and the world's best-known and most-respected soldier. He embodied America's victory and had been able to find compromise and consensus among headstrong Allied leaders where rivalry and bickering predominated. Raised in the solitude of the Kansas plains, he now knew every corner of the globe and had worked intimately with great men of state. He remained comfortable in his own skin, a characteristic that made him a natural communicator with the press, with his fellow military commanders, and especially with the soldiers he sent into battle."[88]

After serving as the President of Columbia University in 1950, he became NATO's Commander in Chief of all allied forces in Europe. On April 6, 1950, Philip W. Porter of the Cleveland Plain Dealer newspaper wrote this about Eisenhower: "There's something about the common sense of his remarks, the clarity of his English, the homey charm of his smile, and the natural humility of the unaffected, un-swellheaded man who has had greatness thrust upon him."[89] After Eisenhower was elected President, he later gave a speech on April 16, 1953, to the American Society of Newspaper Editors in Washington, D.C. The speech became known as "The Chance for Peace."

"The cost of one modern bomber is this: a modern brick school in more than 30 cities. It is two electric power plants, each serving a town of 60,000 population. It is two fine, fully equipped hospitals. It is some 50 miles of concrete highway. We pay for a single fighter plane with a half million bushels of wheat. We pay for a single destroyer with new homes that could have housed more than 8,000 people. This, I repeat, is the best way of life to be found on the road the world has been taking. This is not a way of life at all, in any true sense. Under the cloud of threatening war, it is humanity hanging from a cross of iron."[90]

If the superpowers could agree to arms reductions and limitations: "This government is ready to ask its people to join all nations in devoting a substantial percentage of the savings achieved by disarmament to a fund for world aid and reconstruction. The purpose of this great work would be to help other peoples to develop the underdeveloped areas of the world to stimulate profitable and fair trade, to assist all serving the needs, rather than the fears, of the world."[91]

Eisenhower brought up an important philosophical perspective on how a President should govern the American populace that future Presidents might want to take into consideration. In his Annual Budget Message to Congress on January 17, 1955, he said: "A liberal attitude towards the welfare of people and a conservative approach to the use of their money should be a basis of how one should govern."[92] Having a balanced budget was a priority for Eisenhower.

"In the Eisenhower years, marginal tax rates for the lowest brackets floated at between 20-26%, unlike today, working people at the bottom rungs of the economic ladder paid income taxes in addition to Social Security payroll taxes. But rates were progressive...A head of household who earned $20,000 in 1953, the equivalent of $175,000 today, faced a marginal tax rate of 52%...The top marginal rate was 91% in 1953, on an income of $200,000 or more."[93]

In Eisenhower's address on the Tax Program, March 15, 1954, Eisenhower said: "The good American doesn't ask for favored positions or treatment. Naturally, he wants all fellow citizens to pay their fair share of his taxes, just as he has to do, and he wants every cent collected to be spent wisely and economically. But every real American is proud to carry his share of that burden...I simply do not believe for one second that anyone privileged to live in this country wants someone else to pay his own fair and just cost of the Government."[94]

Fast forward to the present. The Institute on Taxation and Economic Policy says: "For decades, profitable Fortune 500 companies have manipulated the tax system to avoid paying even a dime in tax on billions of dollars in U.S. profits. This ITEP report provides the first comprehensive look at how corporate tax changes under the 2017 Tax Cuts and Jobs Act affect the scale of corporate tax avoidance. The report finds that in 2018, 60 of America's biggest corporations zeroed out their federal income taxes on $79 billion in U.S. pretax income. Instead of paying $16.4 billion in taxes at the 21 percent statutory corporate tax rate, these companies enjoyed a net corporate TAX REBATE of $4.3 billion." Following this paragraph is a list of some of those companies. The CEOs of these companies each made at least $15 to $50 million or more in salary and corporate income and benefits. These dollar amounts are not their total yearly income, just the income received from each company. These three endnote references provide the statistics and the ratios of yearly income of CEOs and their average company workers.[95] [96] [97] Here are a few of the companies that paid no taxes.

Activision Blizzard	Halliburton
AECOM Technology	Honeywell International
Chevron	International Business Machines
Delta Air Lines	Kinder Morgan
Dominion Resources	Netflix
Eli Lilly	Salesforce.com

"Reports from ITEP, as well as various government agencies, had documented how Fortune 500 companies were using legal tax breaks to shelter close to half of their income from federal taxes. But when Congress and the Trump Administration pushed through a technically flawed set of corporate tax changes as part of the Tax Cuts and Jobs Act in December 2017, the new law cut the statutory tax rate to 21% while leaving intact most of the tax breaks that allowed profitable companies to zero out their income taxes."[98] In plain language, they paid nothing in taxes on millions and billions of dollars in income.

How do you citizens in America feel about these facts? You pay your taxes every year. Are these 60 companies, with huge corporate CEO salaries, paying their "fair share," as Eisenhower had stated to America's citizens? Warren Buffet of Berkshire Hathaway fame pays a lower percentage tax rate on his income than the tax rate that the secretaries in his office pay. Do you think that is fair? Remember, politicians wrote these laws.

In March 1953, Eisenhower created the Department of Health, Education, and Welfare. In his Annual Budget to Congress for Fiscal Year 1955, Eisenhower said: "We must make greater and more successful efforts than we have made in the past to strengthen Social Security and improve the health of our citizens. In doing so, we build for the future, and we prove to the watching world that a free Nation can and will find the means, despite the tensions of these times, to progress toward a better society."[99] Social Security is working today but needs to be revised with an aging population while our citizens' health deteriorates.

Eisenhower backed the legislation that created The Civil Rights Act of 1957. In the 1956 Presidential Election, Eisenhower, a Republican, got 40% of the African American vote, the highest percentage ever recorded by a candidate since 1932. Two other major accomplishments were the start of the Interstate Highway System and the St. Lawrence Seaway Act that opened the Great Lakes to ocean-going vessels.

It is true that several controversies made Eisenhower appear weak as a leader: the launch of the Soviet Union's Sputnik I & II and the surprising Intercontinental Ballistic Missile build-up by the USSR. To counter these measures and increase the number of scientists and engineers in the United States, Eisenhower signed the National Defense Education Act into law, and he embraced the creation of the National Aeronautics and Space Agency (NASA), which he signed into law on July 29, 1958. The "space race" and race to build more Intercontinental Ballistic Missiles (ICBMs) for military purposes created the nuclear arms race that eventually put missile silos in 19 states, built many B-47 and B-52 atomic bomb dropping planes, and Polaris missile-launching submarines. The race with the Soviet Union "was on" because of the fears of nuclear annihilation, which was led by those who felt that developing more "might is right" missiles was the pathway to peace.

The fears of Communist firepower changed the positive views of mankind that so many had felt during the early years of the Eisenhower Presidency, where he focused his energy on trying to maintain what was best for the common man's income and welfare. This new armament focus helped lead to new fears nationwide, so much so that in Eisenhower's Presidential farewell address, he said that a "hostile ideology of infinite duration" caused the United States to build "a permanent armaments industry of vast proportions" and that these actions may hurt and degrade our country's democracy. "In the councils of Government, we must guard against the acquisition of unwarranted influence, whether sought or unsought, by the military-industrial complex. The potential for the disastrous rise of misplaced power exists and will persist. We must never let the weight of this combination endanger our liberties or democratic processes." Eisenhower hoped that "all peoples will come together in a peace guaranteed by the binding force of mutual respect and love."[100]

A famous quote from Eisenhower occurred after he left office: "I have no patience with extreme Rightists who call everyone who disagrees with them a Communist, nor with the Leftists who shout that the rest of us are heartless money grabbers."[101]

Eisenhower found that by compromising with the Democrats, he was able to accomplish more for the country by creating more jobs and building our infrastructure with better bridges and highways. His tax policies helped the economy grow, with the rich paying a fairer proportion of their income to help benefit others besides themselves.

During his Presidency, living with positive morals and ethics seemed to have more meaning in an average citizen's life. Most citizens' general outlook was on an "all of us have value and importance" approach rather than big business's approach that "power and corporate wealth have all the solutions to my problems." Using more historical common-sense approaches to today's social and economic problems might be a better approach to achieving solutions for greater long-term stability.

Maybe people should allow themselves to think more about relying on personal remedies instead of assuming that technology will solve most of their dilemmas. Maybe we should start asking ourselves more introspective questions like: "Do I really need that 10th or 20th pair of shoes? How much money or materialism is enough for me to lead a satisfying life? Is overconsumption of food and alcohol a primary activity in my relationships with friends or neighbors? Do possessions or events have to be 'awesome' to satisfy my needs?" A self-analysis of questions like these could help many formulate and build within themself a stronger foundation for emotional peace of mind and happiness.

Look across the country. Does the government or economy seem to be working for the benefit of ALL our citizens? The rich and super-rich make laws and policy decisions to benefit themselves and their friends before reflecting on how their legislative actions will affect the public. Today's economy seems to be based on an aristocratic approach and philosophical belief system, structured in ways that only create greater income inequality.

Don't believe me; just look at all the historical statistics the United States Federal Reserve put out during the last 30-40 years. Much of our chaos occurs when "Capitalism for Me" is the major philosophical guidance imposed by those at the top of our political and economic policy decisions.

Eisenhower failed in the last couple of years of his administration when he stopped listening to the ethical and moral aspects of his own heart and soul and started to listen to the egos of his civilian and military advisors. These advisors influenced Eisenhower to change his original governing ideals based on humility and humanity for all mankind. Instead, he changed his approach and accepted more ego-based, aristocratic philosophies that elevated Americans to be the only exceptional people on this planet, and the only righteous ones with the greatest assets and military might who had the solutions to every problem. I wonder what The Founding Fathers would have said about how this different approach has changed the idealisms on which they founded this country.

Chapter 11

SUMMARY AND ANALYSIS: IS THIS THE END?

In America's form of capitalism, the major goal of economic activity is based first on corporate/business profit and then secondly on growth. Profit and growth capitalism is advocated in America as the best form of economics available and superior to all other forms of structured economies. The biggest cheerleaders of our current economic system are those who make the most money from it and those who hold the greatest economic and political powers in the country.

What are some of these advantages that the rich have gained from American Capitalism that many in the lower and middle classes have not received? In the area of healthcare, the rich have little concern about the cost of health-care expenses. This group of American elites can easily pay for the best colleges and educational opportunities for their children, buy the maximum insurance coverage for everything they own, and ensure their lives for millions of dollars to provide extra bonuses for their families when they die. They can provide any quantity and quality of food for their families and/or visit the fanciest restaurants whenever they wish. They may even have a servant or a hired caterer to shop and cook all their meals for them. People whose incomes are based on large corporate asset profits seem to attract rich marital partners who are usually some of the most beautiful women or most handsome men around.

Suppose you are part of a middle or lower economic class. In that case, you may be viewed by American elites as the pawns on the chessboard that is structured and controlled by them to benefit their economic prosperity. You do not have to believe what I am saying, but you might want to believe Adam Smith, the 1700s founder of the business and economic structure that became American Capitalism. I will rephrase what Adam Smith called the outcome of his economic, capitalistic philosophy: The rich chess kings and queens in America each need 500 working pawns for American Capitalism to mostly benefit themselves.

For more than 40 years, American capitalism has deviated from what occurred in work achievements and social responsibilities during the 1940s to 1970s. If you were not alive during those years you may have no idea what I am talking about. After World War II and Korea, living The American Dream was available to people who wanted to work hard, even those doing manual work, unless you were Black, from other minorities, or women wanting to own a business or have a working career. Hollywood favored the homemaker wife after the war. This is ironic because, during World War II, women successfully filled most jobs that men, then fighting the war, had previously held.

Americans built well-made products, and the average worker could buy a home, pay the bills, and make enough money to put quality food on the family table and set aside some savings. Most mothers could spend time directly educating their children about family responsibilities and social etiquette by teaching them the benefits of developing positive morals and ethics and conveying an understanding of how common sense and rationale could be used throughout children's lives. People understood that there was no personal or family need to follow negative cultist philosophies or play blame games to justify negative social or political ideologies. The historical importance of family unity was trust.

People used face-to-face communication to know and understand each other better. This direct personal activity made resolving arguments or conflicts easier. It was normal for all family members to have responsibilities, which made them more accountable to and interactive with each other. Family-together time was seen as necessary and vital.

But then some things started changing. The well-off members of American society, corporate executives, and Wall Street financiers started preaching that having a greater focus on personal wealth creation and materialistic accumulation should be the true measure of one's success in life and how it would determine one's social image. Banks, credit card companies, and manufacturers bragged that you could have whatever you wanted, even if you did not have the money to buy it. The ability to buy cheap plastic items that looked like objects made from metal and wood became available to the masses. Advertisers often told you that by purchasing cheap plastic substitutes at discount stores, you were saving money. Yes, as absurd as this idea was, Americans who wanted to look financially well off without having the money to buy quality products made the concept of "buy now, pay later" a primary addictive habit. Owning a product became more important than it being of good quality.

Saving money for a future purchase to avoid 10-20% interest rates became a lost practice. Using reason, rationale, and common sense on your life's journey was no longer valued as good philosophies. Wants now became Needs. Owning more and doing more of everything, no matter what everything was, became a person's new pathway to status and social recognition. These new behaviors justified people's keeping up with or exceeding the Joneses' image.

The ability to sign on the dotted line showed prosperity whether you needed the product or not. This new idea of "wealth imaging" in society helped magnify larger differences between your social class and lower socio-economic classes, even if your wallet was empty of cash and you could not afford an ice cream cone. This imaging created great overspending and massive debt that could take decades to pay off because of high-interest rates. But what the hell? Looking well-off seemed more important than being financially responsible within your family.

This increased delineation of class ranking started dominating all forms of personal communications and purchases in American Capitalism. This new public image was presented and magnified by television and advertising marketers: buy my corporate interpretation of what having a "normal and appropriate" lifestyle should look like to justify acquiring their products or following their advice. Following the crowd-buying practices created super-wealthy corporate powerhouses. Then, companies increased their development of obsolescent manufacturing techniques. They could also place nearer future expiration dates on products, like pharmaceutical drugs, that gave them shorter viability usage.

Then came high-tech. Addictive behaviors and the loss of historical common sense accelerated like never seen in American history. Social media platforms allowed anyone to market anything or say anything, no matter how false, vile, corrupt, or degrading it was. Political leaders and cult-like groups drew tens of millions into their webs of lies and deceptions. The concept of truth could be anything anyone wanted it to be. This proliferation of propaganda, in one instance, resulted in the United States Capitol Building in Washington D.C. being illegally invaded and damaged by riotous protesters to try and stop a legal Presidential succession procedure. An event like this had not occurred in America's history.

There are countries in the world that use Capitalism in their economic structure, but it is not like American Capitalism. Other countries, like those in the Scandinavian region, use some of the basics of Adam Smith's philosophy but adapt many of their laws and regulations to provide more benefits for their entire population. Instead of putting multi-billion/trillion-dollar companies first in line for tax relief, corporate welfare, or tax loopholes, these countries instituted universal health care, mandatory savings and retirement programs, and longer worker-paid vacations, to mention a few. They do not allow manipulative pharmaceutical advertising on television, nor do they allow political candidates to run political campaigns for years before elections. Parental leave for newborn children, quality childcare, and free student education were added.

Advancing new government policies to benefit citizens is sometimes easier when, like in the Scandinavian countries, there are more than two political parties. Compromising becomes mandatory to accomplish anything, especially when other political parties are not trying to mandate philosophies that limit voters to accept only one way of thinking.

There are many hindrances to starting a new political party in America. Rules and regulations established by the two major parties in states and nationally have made it very difficult to establish a viable third party.

Historically, the most successful method has been to start a new party in small towns, then advance to the city level, then the county. It takes a while for voters to understand other political perspectives and ideologies. When people hear about other political perspectives, they question them.

America's current two political parties are monopolies that trade power back and forth with each other after elections. Why compromise with your opponent's party when your party is not in power? You can just wait until your party gets back in power and then enact new rules and benefits for your political tribe. You can then investigate whomever you want in the other party to see if their activities were illegal or corrupt.

American political ads have also become more abusive and hateful. The party not in power tells the American people that the party in power has policies that are failures. They tell the public that real change can only occur when their party is in power. Politicians then start behaving like spoiled, demanding children, pouting, blaming, and pointing fingers at everyone else but themselves for social or governmental problems.

INFLATION

One reason for inflation is when personal wants have more priority and justification in one's life than personal needs. This type of behavior repeats itself throughout history when a society's excessive display of wealth, held in the hands of a minority of the population, reaches a certain reactionary point in the general public's eyes. The rest of the population then tries to mimic the materialistic over-accumulation exhibited by elitist actors, singers, sports stars, or flamboyant industrialists. Average consumers unrealistically conclude that by flaunting smaller wealth-like behaviors, they might feel like they have created a personal connection with those members of an elite class they admire. Many people enjoy trying to live in this fantasyland. But in the process, they may lose their moral compass and negatively affect their family's economic stability. Isn't that what you see happening to many "stars" in tabloids or in public displays of corruption?

Another aspect of addictive behavior is when people believe, without verification, that the propaganda that corporate advertisers tell them is the truth. This belief could involve something as simple as over-buying or over-consuming commercial products that are bad for one's health. Or it can involve people irrationally following certain politicians to the point where those politicians are seen as their personal gods or saviors who are willing to eliminate any opposing person or party that claims a different perspective. Accepting lies and misinformation from companies and politicians as absolute truths seems to have become a capitalistic and political normality today.

There is an aspect of inflation that very few people, especially politicians, want to discuss, which is waste. America is one of planet Earth's biggest, if not the biggest, waste producers. People's addictions to synthetic fabrics and "plastic fantastic everything" are overusing fossil fuels and helping to destroy the oceans and eliminate many varieties of the flora and fauna that live here. Drive down any highway and look along the sides of the road. Plastics are in fences, trees, farmlands, and city streets. Do you know how long it takes for Styrofoam to decompose? In a landfill it takes 500 years. A recent study at the University of Technology Sydney found that humans ingest microplastics equivalent to the size of a credit card every week. Yearly world plastic production: 882 billion pounds. Only about 9% of plastics are recycled, with 91% dumped into the environment.

If our government really wanted to protect the health of its citizens, why aren't they banning more plastics to prevent them from harming us, the planet, and the future generations of our children and grandchildren? Plastic grocery bags have been banned in about 100 countries. The United Kingdom has banned plastic plates, straws, plastic cutlery, and Styrofoam food packaging containers. Who is paying off our politicians not to pass legislation to ban many toxic products that can last for centuries?

Realistically, most people don't care because if they cared, they wouldn't buy or use products that contain these compounds. Here is an example of typical American behavior. People eat fast food to quickly satisfy their taste buds and hunger. After eating at a fast-food restaurant, many people put their plastic utensils and Styrofoam packaging in the company's garbage cans. This out-of-sight, out-of-mind activity makes them feel like they might have done their responsibility to the store, but they are not acting responsibly toward the environment.

What about all those clothes and products that people buy and then throw away or keep in storage boxes forever that come from coal, gas, or crude oil? It is not only the gasoline that you put into your cars, the type of fuel that heats your homes, or the electricity that is made from using carbon-based fuels that pollute the environment. The following are some of the products that come from crude oil: acrylics, microfibers, nylon, rayon, spandex, polyester, neoprene, vinyl siding, and many more.

Plastics are also produced from natural gas, feedstocks from natural gas processing, and feedstocks derived from crude oil refining. (Feedstock is a petrochemical terminology word that has nothing to do with cattle or human food.) The more products made from crude oil and natural gas that you buy, the higher the price of gasoline and home heating fuel. It is simple supply and demand economics. People's excessive buying habits make everything cost more. Americans love wearing mental horse blinders to avoid seeing and feeling the impact that their habits have on everyone and everything around them.

Inflation can also increase depending on what foods you buy. People in America waste a lot of food. American food waste is over 80 billion pounds per year, about 219 pounds of wasted food for every man, woman, and child. Food waste costs 218 billion dollars a year. Wasted food takes up more space in landfills than anything else. The United States could feed all its malnourished children with the food Americans throw away. Over-consumption of food and the waste of food that is thrown away by both families and businesses contribute to inflation. Ignorance can be infectious.

Remember what happened during the COVID-19 pandemic. At the beginning of Covid, people panicked, rushed to grocery stores, and bought everything they could. Then, there was a period when people weren't going out because places of employment, restaurants, and other stores were closed. People stayed home. Why go out and get sick? Unemployment skyrocketed.

Months later came a period when everyone wanted to buy everything, but by then, the supply chain was broken with COVID-19 having shut down large factories and food production all over the planet. When supply chains are broken, it takes a lot of time to repair them. This resulted in a buying panic to satisfy latent buying habits and addictions. It became a simple under-supply and over-demand situation. A do more, buy more, waste more series of activities created greater increases in inflation. The over-consuming behaviors of citizens and the increases in America's debt by politicians in their attempt to appease the populace and keep themselves in power helped create even more debt burdens and inflation for the country. This behavior constantly repeats itself, and no one cares.

There is another reason why inflation occurs. The United States has commodity trading platforms in a couple of major cities. These businesses allow for trading products like heating oil, gasoline, crude oil, corn, wheat, soybeans, sugar, currencies, gold, silver, hogs, cattle, lumber, United States Treasury bonds, bills, and stock indexes, to name a few. These platforms trade futures and options contracts for each commodity. Futures contracts are agreements to buy or sell a predetermined amount of a commodity at a specific price before a specific date in the future. You can buy or sell your purchased futures contract within seconds, minutes, hours, days, or years after you have purchased it. This is a simple definition, but obviously, the activity is more complex.

The value of the contracts traded has very little to do with the price you pay for the contract. You may only have to "put up" (pay upfront) a couple of thousand dollars to own a contract valued at $100,000. The ratio is different for each type of commodity contract. Commodity trading is more speculative in nature, with the possibility of either making or losing a great deal of money over various periods of time.

The prices paid for a commodity futures contract, and the amount of interest in a particular commodity are not different from what happens in the general consumer world when you buy items in a grocery store or at the gas pump. When more futures contract traders keep bidding the price of a commodity higher because they think there may be a current or a future shortage of gasoline, corn, sugar, etc., next week or in a couple of months, they can overpower the ability of the traders who are selling the same product's contracts. Demand is exceeding supply. The same thing happens when prices are falling, like during the Pandemic when gas prices at the pump collapsed because people weren't driving much and refilling their gas tanks, which increased the supply of gas. More supply, less usage, lower prices. But many people can't seem to comprehend the results of the opposite scenario, that greater demand creates less supply and higher prices for everything. The greatest economic benefits go to those who know best how to manipulate the financial and commodity markets.

If you watch TV channels like CNBC, Bloomberg, or Fox Business, every day that the stock markets are open, the stock futures markets signal what will happen before the U.S. stock markets open at 9:30 am Eastern Time. Some people do not realize that brokerage companies operate 24 hours a day around the globe, buying and selling stocks, bonds, currencies, and commodities. Prices can fluctuate wildly with stocks and commodities while most Americans are sleeping.

Here is the significant thing to understand about big financial markets in the world today: most of the trading in financial markets is done by Artificial Intelligence computers that are often programmed to respond to minor changes in worldwide market sentiments or data, or even rumors, in fractions of a second. This is faster than it takes you to blink your eyes. And just as fast as buying more of a product like corn or a financial product, these computers can reverse their trading and massively sell the same commodity product, stock, or stock indexes.

With commodity futures, you can both buy and sell the same product at the same time, provided they are bought in different contract months. Anything to try and make a profit. This is why you have seen the Dow Jones Industrial average go up and down hundreds, even thousands of points in a single day. This is what AI computers can easily do to increase wealth among those who program and control the machines. The same goes for soybeans, sugar, orange juice, or any other commodity. Rich investors and speculators who drive prices up or down in the futures commodity markets for quick short-term profits make the prices you pay at the pump go up or down, even when the commodity markets' price movements result from false rumors or accelerated speculative desires to make greater profits. But in the end, whatever direction prices move, advances in prices generally come faster and last longer than price declines. Increased prices in gasoline go into effect at the pump almost immediately but declines in prices may feel like they take a long time. It's how the pricing game operates to benefit the sellers.

Here is another financial statistic that most average investors may not like. During 2022, the stock market was down 15-35% or more for the average investor. But the rich "short sellers" who drove the market down had monetary gains in 2022 of $300 billion. You lose, they win, and average investors are usually excluded from participating in this market trading game because they are told that a person needs to be wealthy to afford big losses in case a selling short strategy goes against them. When the markets go down, a lot of rich people smile while Average Joes are sad and depressed, and in that emotional state, they often blame a scapegoated President's policies instead of the AI computer villains who own the computers that create many scary market sell-offs.

The last factor I will mention may be the most important. The average citizen may not understand who is pulling the real strings behind the scenes, which results in inflation hurting one's personal economic status. The Federal Reserve controls interest rates. They are the only governmental agency for which there is no check and balance accountability from any other authority over the decisions they make. No President, Congress, Courts, or voting powers of the American people can regulate or veto the policies or decisions the Federal Reserve makes concerning the American economy and how their decisions affect your personal economic status. As was explained in a previous chapter, the Federal Reserve was created in 1913 by the rich for the benefit of the rich, who wanted assurances that no other governmental authority could interfere with the greater wealth-building activities of those already wealthy and in power. A small group of people own most of the world's wealth. Jerome Powell, the Chairman of the Federal Reserve, worked as an investment banker for the Carlyle

Group, a global private equity firm, and was nominated by President Donald Trump to that Chairmanship position. Powell became the first chairman who had no formal training in economics. Some estimate his net worth to be 20-50 million dollars.

Here is a simple explanation of why gasoline, food, etc., were cheaper in 2019-2020 and the stock market soared. Powell dropped interest rates to practically zero and held them there for a long period of time to stimulate the economy. Big, wealthy investors and investment companies loved this maneuver as the stock market exploded with huge increases in market valuations because of cheap borrowing rates.

But later, after COVID cases started receding, Americans and others around the world went on a buying spree where the demand for products and inadequate supply chain management caused inflation to soar. Powell found himself forcing interest rates higher and higher over time, but these small increases in interest rates were done too slowly. These small interest rate increases resulted in Powell's actions being disregarded by large investment traders who saw his actions as insignificant to curb over-buying. Powell's hesitancy for larger and quicker interest rate hikes increased further speculation in commodity and stock markets. Inflation kept increasing as people kept over-buying, and that mostly hurt average Americans. Powell was then forced to raise interest rates by greater amounts more quickly. Average Americans then saw big increases in mortgage and credit card interest rates, with some rates doubling. Inflation causes almost all product prices to increase. But wages could not keep up with these borrowing rates, so consumer debt went to all-time highs. Simultaneously, employment exploded higher, and the unemployment rate dropped to 3.4%, the lowest since May of 1969.

It was the "not responsible to anyone" Federal Reserve that started way too late to increase interest rates when they should have increased rates sooner. Yes, many people are very upset and are complaining about this increase in interest rates, but they forget that mortgage rates over the last 60 years have varied between 2.65% and 18.63% with the 30-year average being 7.72%. It seems that when Federal Fund rates are near 0% with mortgages under 3% people lose their minds with overzealous spending, greater credit card and debt accumulation, and stock market speculation.

There are around 543 million credit cards in the United States as of 1/1/2024. The average number of credit cards by generation is: 2.1 for a person in Generation Z, 3.4 for Millennials, 4.4 for Generation X, 4.6 for Baby Boomers, and 3.4 for those in the Silent Generation.

LIBERALS AND CONSERVATIVES

With current society's minimal interest in history, large numbers of people can be more easily manipulated with the same tactics that have been periodically used by companies and politicians for centuries. When the average citizen's life starts to suffer morally and economically, scape-goating others generally follows. Ask any addictive behavioral psychologist or psychiatrist for confirmation on this activity. Denial of personal responsibility by blaming anyone but themselves is at the core of an addictive behavior. People heartily desire someone else or something external to themselves to be the cause of their self-created problems. Blame it on the liberals, blame it on the conservatives, blame it on a company's product, or just blame everything negative in your life on the President.

In the 1920s and 1930s, many people in Germany liked Hitler. He was only doing what other corrupt governmental leaders have done throughout history. Naïve people have followed and become true believers of Hitleresque-type leaders who have preached that they would do whatever it took to "make their country great again."

When politicians use the words conservative or liberal when speaking to the American public, they try to make themselves sound like everything they believe in is the correct ideology that is best for everyone in America. Conservative or liberal political ideologies have little to do with personal ideologies concerning a person's physical or mental health, their moral or ethical decisions in life, or making the best choices for their children, grandparents, or themselves.

A politically conservative politician's life can be filled with excessive liberal attitudes and practices. A conservative politician can be obese, be an alcoholic, have an interest in porn, have marital affairs, be hateful of blacks, or oppose other nationalities wanting to become American citizens. They might call themselves Christian or Jewish followers for display purposes but completely disregard the basic moral and ethical religious philosophies of Christ, Moses, or Abraham in their daily lives.

The same is true for politicians who declare they follow liberal political philosophies. Many liberals may advocate being progressive in health and wellness for themselves, but their health-conscious attitude does not always translate to other liberal-thinking behaviors. Being too liberal can create chaos by letting people act out ideologies that are overly extreme. For example, a liberal can say that everyone has the right to do anything for or to themselves as long as it does not break the law. This is the opposite of what the New and Old Testament or other religions have taught.

Many liberals become silent observers when they claim that people should not investigate, point out, or rationalize what other liberal-minded people look like or how they are behaving. Many liberals believe that everyone should just accept each person as an asset for the welfare of society while disregarding how a liberal person's unhealthy moral or ethical lifestyle may be negatively affecting the welfare and/or health of themselves, their family, or the nation.

Any type of extremism in a culture, whether it be conservatively or liberally based, distorts the desire for people to come together and create compromise and good physical and economic health for everyone.

AMERICA'S HEALTH

As stated earlier in this book, obesity is crippling the strength of the country. Greater dependence on health professionals and facilities, higher insurance rates for everyone, being less able to physically participate in many types of jobs, and not being able to serve in the military because of health issues are just a few of the reasons why our country is becoming weaker. Many societies around the world eat healthier, are more physically active, and are happier with their lives than Americans. Let's look at a simple statistic concerning America's physical health today. Our obesity

rate is at least 40%. How does this compare to other industrialized societies around the world? These are the current obesity rates in Norway
(25%), Germany (19%), France (17%), Sweden (17%), China (15%),
Switzerland (12%), and Japan (4%). Most of these countries are major
competitors of the United States. What is even sadder is looking at pictures
of our children today compared to other children around the globe. American children are not the smartest, healthiest, most obedient, or reasonably
minded children in the world, but they may be some of the most stressed-
out and obese among children in major industrialized countries.

Many of America's children, teenagers, and young adults are more
spoiled and catered to by their parents than in any previous generation. A
parent who feels that they should safeguard their children against all the
evils and criminal behaviors on American streets by being overprotective
does not seem to fear giving their children unlimited access to the brainwashing abilities of evil people, religious fanatics, and "pseudo-authori-
tarian truth tellers" on the Internet and social media platforms through their
"smart(?)" phones and computers.

America's current "spare setting restrictions and spoil the child" ideologies and the acceptance of sit-in-place technology-focused lifestyles are
producing overweight and obese children and adults by the tens of millions. With few standards of decency or moral limitations on personal behaviors in our "my truth is whatever I want it to be" society, many Americans become open to accepting greater behavioral decadence as part of a
normal lifestyle.

HEALTHCARE

In 2022, the United States' healthcare spending per person was around
$13,500, yet America is not very healthy compared to many other similar
industrialized countries in the world. Concerning 2022 statistics, misplaced logic might suggest that these other nations must have spent far
greater amounts of money to develop and maintain healthier citizens than
those in the United States. That assumption is wrong! Other nations spend
a lot less money: Australia around $9600, Canada around $8500, Germany

spent around $8000, Sweden $6500, France $5500, South Korea $5500, and Japan $5200 as examples. (Organization for Economic Cooperation Development's 2022 Health Statistics.)

There is also a huge disparity in medical administrative expenditures in the United States versus that of some of our trading partners. The United States spends about $1000 in administrative costs per citizen annually. What about these other countries? Germany and France spent about $300, Canada about $200, Australia $150, South Korea $125, Sweden $100, and Japan $80. (OECD) Take the example of the U.S. at $1000 vs. Japan at $80. Multiply just this one yearly cost difference by the hundreds of millions of people in America, and you would produce huge savings in costs if administrative expenses were more standardized and computerized.

Another reason why the United States spends so much more on healthcare coverage is the result of its for-profit, Capitalism for Me healthcare system. Many other countries use a Capitalism for Us universal health care coverage form of providing medical care. America has huge numbers of devout, heavily compensated Capitalism for Me believers and justifiers who are investment corporations, campaign-funded politicians, medical providers (doctors, therapists, etc.), lawyers, and insurance companies, to name a few, where profit outcomes are generally ranked as more important than healthcare outcomes. What is the proof of this statement?

Just look at recent pictures of people on the streets in all these other countries that provide Capitalism for Us healthcare for its citizens. Their people are thinner, more physically active, eat healthier diets, take greater healthcare responsibility for their elders, produce healthier varieties of foods, and eat far fewer junk foods than Americans. But the important fact here is that in many other countries, the primary focus of health practitioners is on the total health outcomes of the citizens in their country while receiving a reasonable salary instead of building large American medical practices that elevate the practitioners to elite monetary and corporate hierarchies. In America, corporations mostly choose power and financial outcomes over healthy population results.

The current American healthcare system is not decreasing the ways by which citizens are more aggressively gravitating toward addictive behaviors that are negatively affecting their lives. America has a healthcare system that is treating the end results of its citizens' personal, abusive behaviors but is not treating the causes that created their negative health situations. It is an "after the damage is done" form of medical care that often creates a need for more specialized healthcare providers who wind up treating one failed organ, one broken body part, or one disease. Classical, health-focused, general practitioners are disappearing.

After a patient's abusive behavior has created a complex and interconnected negative state of being in both their body and mind, any approach toward healing should encompass total body/mind remedies. What is missing in our educational system is comprehensive preventive care instructions and remedies from local qualified educators starting from when a child can first read, which can be advanced and broadened until they become adults. If children are taught early in their lives how to live and stay healthy, they will need less medical care later in life. Shouldn't preventive healthcare be the foundation of all American healthcare options?

When I was growing up in the 1950s and early 1960s, our family doctor would make sure that all the children under his care received their vital vaccinations, would advise parents how certain poor eating behaviors would cause their children problems in the future, and he would ask parents if the children were getting enough sleep and physical exercise. At times he would come to patients' homes, check if the child's living conditions were appropriate for their good health and give parents easy-to- read medical information so they could learn how positive health habits would increase a child's ability to live a long and healthy life.

I would call these approaches "classical medicine," starting at birth and continuing throughout a person's life to provide the best health and holistic medical guidance for good long-term outcomes. Compare those old-fashioned, classical forms of healthcare to what you are experiencing today. Is today's medical approach making you healthier and happier?

Many American parents have also created paranoia, apprehension, and fear among their children by restricting their freedom to explore many avenues of self-educating themselves by exploring their surrounding environments. They pamper, spoil, and buy a lot of their children's love and attention with toys, electronic gadgets, large allowances, and adult-style benefits instead of guidance and inspiration. Friending your children is not the same as parenting your children. Today, Mom has become Mary, and Dad has become Jim, and in this process, parents are treating their children as if they were equals. Many parents have given their children as young as 3-5 the privilege and responsibility to vote on what the family does, what they buy, eat, and where they go without the child being able to understand the mental, emotional, or health implications of what they are choosing: for example, choosing candy vs. apples.

Don't feed or give the children what they need; feed or give them what they want. If they finish all the food on their plate, give them a little trophy as a reward to add to all their other trophies from events like hitting a perched ball on a post or kicking a miniature soccer ball into a net from 3-4 feet away. Even at the grade school level, many children grow up with "what's in it for me" attitudes when asked to do a simple chore, feeling that everything is negotiable with their parents.

Try this. If you need to punish them for something they did, take away their cell phones for a couple of weeks, and you might see how spoiled or bratty the loss of their addictive phones makes them. Maybe they will feel less stressed, get less bullied by fellow students, or they may even read a book for fun instead of watching a mass murder movie.

I can hear what you are thinking. "My innocent little children need their phones for emergencies or to call home." Parents and grandparents, did you have your own old, personal dial phone and phone number in your bedroom at home when you were 6-12 years old? Did you survive all the crime and mayhem in the places where you lived? So, parents, why not give them a simple flip phone to use for emergencies or to call home?

Giving them a $300-1500 fancy, unlimited-everything smartphone only sets them up to demand a $40-50,000 car when they graduate from high school. What are you going to do to keep them happy after college, buy them their own fully furnished home?

Maybe parents are just too busy making money and having a complex and entertaining social life to spend more time with their children. Maybe they feel that delegating their parental instruction to others will somehow miraculously fill the historically important aspect of parenthood bonding with their children as they mature. Are daycare helpers teaching your young children right from wrong behaviors and feeding them the proper foods to build their little bodies like you yourself could do at home? If you can't properly take care of your children's health and well-being from birth to adulthood, why are you having children? Maybe you might be more attentive and caring about a pet dog or cat.

As children get older, if they do not learn how to cook healthy meals, clean and maintain a home, know how to balance income and expenditures, and learn from hard knocks and disappointing events in their life, they may wind up with an attitude like: "Why do I have to know how to do all this crap? I'll just make a lot of money like my parents did and hire someone else to cook my food, clean and maintain my home, and raise my kids. This will allow me to have more time to do whatever I want for myself." A child's first and continuous example of learning how to behave comes from their parents. It's also sort of a historical Christian or Jewish thing, isn't it?

RELIGION

There is a problem in America with too many people claiming to believe in a Christian-based religion but failing to live and abide by the basic moral and ethical fundamentals of that religion. Many people seem to believe that following new pseudo, almost anything is acceptable, forms of Christianity are equivalent to what Christ taught. But they aren't.

Just saying you are a Christian is one reality. Following Christ's teachings and philosophies is a different reality. Portraying an image of being a good Christian by dressing up and looking prim and proper as you enter a church has little to do with acting like an ethical and moral Christian in all aspects of your daily life. If Christ's inspiration and guidance are everywhere, what is the difference if you dress right to attend and communicate through prayer in a church or don't dress-up and pray at home? Maybe you feel that God pays more attention to a group of nicely clothed believers praying together. Or is it that attending with a group might have more positive social and status implications than religious ones.

If someone claims that their victory in a sporting contest was inspired by their belief in Jesus or God because He loved them in His special way, is it really God that made them win? For example, if the winner of a boxing or tennis match says God or Jesus inspired them to win the contest, and the loser thought the same thing, does that mean that God is picking winners and losers depending on His mood during the event?

If Christianity or your religion says that killing is wrong, then people who want to stop abortions should also want to ban capital punishment. Would Christ say that killing innocent men, pregnant women, and children who are collateral damage from any country's bombs or missiles is a morally permissible activity? What about when civilians are targeted?

When we dropped atomic bombs on Hiroshima and Nagasaki near the end of World War II, we killed a lot of babies in the wombs of innocent, noncombatant mothers. Many American leaders and military chieftains cheered "whatever it took" to kill the enemy for the United States to win the war. Our destruction of those population centers and the resulting deaths of all the young and unborn children in the process weren't even thought of as a negative "thou shalt not kill" activity by our leaders.

What most people in America don't know is that prior to dropping atomic bombs on those two Japanese cities, on the night of March 9-10, 1945, 279 American bomber planes dropped napalm bombs on Tokyo and totally burned to the ground 16 square miles of central Tokyo, Japan. Napalm bombs are a form of jellied gasoline bombs that, when they reach the ground and explode, burn everything on or near what the jellied gas touches. This one-night raid was the most destructive bombing mission in human history. Over 100,000 civilians died, and 1 million were left homeless. But today, many Americans think that aborting the fetus of a pregnant woman who was forcefully raped numerous times by a stranger or aborting a fetus that will not survive birth are crimes against humanity. Is murdering a person of a different color or race excusable in God's eyes?

Maybe you feel that in matters of excessive food consumption, obsessive sexual activity, porn, and immoral or unethical business practices, religious teachings should be disregarded or ignored. With this type of exclusionary thinking, people might feel free to prioritize financial gains and hedonistic behaviors over any spiritual or religious belief systems.

Those who advocate Anti-Christian behaviors in our society might be some of the food, tobacco, and alcohol providers and the legal and illegal providers of drugs and porn. Internet companies that provide people of all ages examples of how to disrespect and disobey the fundamentals of a Christian-based religion on their platforms are also responsible. We cannot call America a Christian nation if we, as individuals, accept and participate in all the readily available anti-Christian propaganda on the Internet that brainwashes people into believing that any type of behavior is acceptable. Think of what all this propaganda is doing to our country's children who are being targeted from birth through adulthood with false, negative, sexist, and violent activities portrayed as fun or acceptable behaviors. Becoming or saying that you are a member of an organized religion is your choice. But being a hypocrite by acting disrespectful of the tenets, morals, and ethics of that religion is arrogant.

The older and richer elites of a society who glorify money over virtue will always try to influence the young, no matter what their age. Throughout history, it has been an expressive way to achieve more power over others and produce greater financial gains for oneself.

A big question that everyone should be asking themselves is: What are my priorities in life? Before thinking about your family, finances, or country, you need to think about your own body and mental framework. If you are not sufficiently fit and healthy, you won't be able to properly care for your family. In fact, if you have made poor choices for yourself, you may become a burden to your family for years, just trying to keep you alive. But then again, American families send their parents and grandparents to nursing homes or assisted living facilities to let someone else be their family caregiver. Many families falsely believe that just paying for a parent or grandparent's nursing home is the best way to express how much they truly love them. Go visit many of these senior facilities, and you will find out how many children dump their parents there and rarely, if ever, go back to visit them. Most families around the world do not treat their seniors this way. They treat their seniors as valued family members with great wisdom who can be beneficial examples for their children to learn humility and parental respect.

EDUCATION

Modern American educational formats have lost focus on what learning methods will help develop a student's mind and body so that they will want to create unity and stability within themselves and with others.

Teachers should help students learn how to achieve harmony and compromise with others before they enter the adult world. For centuries, a Classical Education, which Our Founding Fathers experienced at home and when they went to school, helped to create a fundamental structure on how to develop one's mind to achieve a greater understanding of human nature and how to avoid those forces and ideas that could corrupt and distort their personal development.

The types of education many of the Founding Fathers received gave people a more balanced approach to dealing with repetitive, negative historical patterns. Here, I will mention two philosophers whom many of Our Founding Fathers intensely studied in their youth and throughout their lives before they formed the new American Government.

Plato wrote that people who desire to participate in the political arena should be chosen because of their intellect and educational aptitudes, and those individuals should devote themselves to enhancing wisdom among the citizens. Aristotle wrote that governments can be created for either the welfare of the people or the welfare of the rulers. Plato also said that besides focusing on positive ethics and morality on how citizens are educated, it must produce citizens who are capable of healthy emotional responses that are in harmony with reason.

In the high school I attended, where the teachers based their courses on a classical education approach, I took four years of Latin translating Caesar, Virgil, and Cicero. In 1963, during my freshman year, in one course we spent an entire year reading and analyzing Plato's "Republic" and two other philosophical works. During my freshman year there was an art class where we created paintings, drawings, and mosaics, and we cut and sculped wood slabs on both sides for two-color woodblock printing of our own self-drawn portraits. As a high school sophomore, there was a biology class where we were tested on how much we had learned from topics like the chemistry of human aerobic respiration and how to diagram the Krebs cycle that takes place in the cell mitochondria by consuming oxygen, producing carbon dioxide and water as waste products, and converting ADP to abundant energy.

In an American history class, we were required to type up and submit a comprehensive outline of everything the teacher taught us in his class, adding at least an additional 30% of extra historical material that we had to research on our own and submit it with our outline. I learned more from my chemistry teacher in our junior year class than I received in my first year of chemistry in college.

In all my classes, the students were taught the value and importance of living a moral and ethical life and the significance of being a responsible citizen to both family and country. There was a heavy emphasis on learning about and understanding the development of American history and how it might affect us today. Yes, this was a private school that my parents could not afford, but I was given a scholarship from a benefactor because of my grade school class achievements and science projects. I later learned that the education I had received was like much of what the Founding Fathers learned in school, but their depth of subject matter was even more comprehensive and demanding than mine.

Suppose a student or citizen can understand how history tends to repeat itself and they use this rationality and reasoning as a basis for how they make their political and lifestyle choice. In that case, they might recognize the historically negative biases that are often repeated which have often led to failed societies and governments. When the population in a country becomes naïve about the past and does not pay attention to what is going on in the present, they tend to make even bigger mistakes in their daily lives. As a result, it becomes easier for them to fall for the latest extremist attitudes and sensationalist propaganda from current political leaders, corporate advertisers, cult groups, and monopolistic media platforms.

In the early to mid-1700s in America, Christian theologians empha-sized that a Classical education, like I have described, was in tune with being a good Christian. What is in tune with being a good Christian today?

What are children learning from today's anything is acceptable, nega-tive Internet propaganda? Is it in tune with being a good Christian? There are other aspects of education that could be adopted in our school systems that could serve as practical guides to help children deal with life's challenges. One of those could be to provide our youth with a nutritional education so they have some type of healthy framework to use as they grow into adulthood. These classes should be developed by schools work-ing with local dietitians and nutritional consultants based on local and eth-nic food customs, what nutritious foods are readily available, and a fam-ily's economic ability to provide them. Having a comprehensive physical education program to maintain bone, muscle, and organ development would also be of great benefit to all young children and teens.

Obese and/or indifferent parents might object to classes emphasizing a healthy nutritional approach. They may object with comments like: "No one is going to tell me how to raise my children," or saying, "My children can make their own choices of what to eat and what they want to do phys-ically." You've got to be kidding me. Do you think that children who have little to no nutritional education can make healthy choices about what they should eat? Left alone and medically uninformed, children will eat what the TV and the Internet have been telling them to eat since they were born.

Maybe both children and adults would make healthier choices for them-selves if they knew more about "epigenetic inheritance." Most parents do not understand the consequences of paternal trans-evolutionary epigenetic inheritance. As a result, they wonder why their children are unhealthy with obesity, high blood pressure, diabetes, or early signs of heart problems – the same problems their parents are having. It could be that parents don't want them to know, or maybe they don't really care.

Maybe bringing back Home Economics might be another good idea. Learning Home Economics began in America after the Revolutionary War. Both parents and teachers took pride in instructing children and teen-agers in numerous fundamental activities that helped create a greater sense of personal growth. These activities developed from America's acceptance of Enlightenment Era thinking prior to the Revolutionary War.

The explosion in the consumption of fast food by America's youth says a lot about how both our school systems and today's parents are not teaching children basic nutritional information and food preparation. The loss of Home Economics in schools was a great loss for America because it helped create more stability in a family's physical health, showed the importance of family responsibilities, taught how to deal with inflationary factors, how to save money for emergencies, and the rewarding benefits that are created by selfless cooperation among all family members.

There is another educational experience that both children and families might consider having. This involves trying to make a stronger connection with the Earth that keeps humanity alive. During World War II, when food became expensive and scarce because of the war, the Federal Government encouraged families to grow "liberty gardens" for their families and friends. Today, when you shop at many grocery stores, what do you get? Many vegetables that look good but are tasteless, chemically fertilized and sprayed with, who knows what, petrochemicals or fungicides, and meat with unknown backgrounds from filthy feeding lots. If you were alive in the 1940s to 1960s and ate fruits and vegetables that were more locally produced, you could taste the difference between what was grown then and now. Today's vegetables have been genetically modified not to enhance flavor but for the ability to have longer viability during transport.

Personal and smaller-scale gardening elicits tranquility and connections with the soil of Mother Earth. Gardens can be set up in a couple of days and be made almost weed-free if you know the right methods. I can hear the parental excuses. "I have no time" (but maybe you have time for unhealthy behaviors.) "I don't want to get my hands dirty; it could damage my manicured fingernails." (I guess you've never heard of gloves or having your children do most of the manual work.) "I hate encountering bugs." (There are organic sprays and organic ways to prevent them.) "My husband spends hours cutting the grass, trimming the hedges, etc. Outside of the house is his domain." American pioneering women would have never left the East coast of the United States and created the country we now have with an attitude like that. If you can't grow some of your own food, try visiting local farmers' markets. Some of these markets even exist indoors in the winter, and some markets often sell locally raised meats. Churches often have cooperative gardening ventures for their members. Try finding organic foods grown without synthetic chemicals.

Encountering and dealing with problems, sorrows, abuses, and even deaths throughout your lifetime can make you stronger if you accept negative experiences as important learning opportunities. One thing that helped my body and mind was experiencing forms of military training and conditioning. One of the great things about a morally based, balanced military education is that it helps develop a person's mental and physical acuity to overcome hardships and difficulties while still focusing on bigger and more important objectives beyond the school environment. Many aspects of a military education develop around historical remembrances, maybe even some that occurred within your own family.

There are many ways that children can be reared. (Rearing means properties acquired by children from parents who taught them how to behave as honored members of society and their families.) If you nourish your children with a proper diet, for example, they might live longer and be healthier than children whose parents set no dietary boundaries for their children.

If schools and parents taught students to be both mentally and physically aware of the importance of good health, life would be very different for most Americans. But corporate advertising tries to convince you that you should not limit your desire to do, eat, or drink anything you want. But those same corporate advertisers are not going to be at your bedside in a hospital years later after you have a heart attack from blocked arteries or a stroke from the "I can eat or do whatever I want" diet and lifestyle you had chosen for yourself.

Historically, education within families started the moment a child was born and continued until a certain level of maturity was reached within each child. Today's modern society has the mother quickly get back to her external job as she assumes that others will be the responsible influencers.

POLITICS

We need to understand a couple of historical facts about the Founding Fathers and relate this information to how we view our current politicians. Do you know the ages of our 1700s American patriots when the Declaration of Independence was signed?

These individuals transformed our country by adopting new dimensions for political independence and social justice. Monroe was 18, Hamilton was 21, Betsy Ross was 24, Madison was 25, Jefferson (who wrote most of the Declaration of Independence) was 33, John Adams was 40, Daniel Boone was 41, Paul Revere was 41, and Washington was 44.

Do you know the ages of some of our country's transformational Presidents when they took office? Washington was 57, Adams was 61, Jefferson was 57, Madison was 57, Monroe was 58, Lincoln was 52, Teddy Roosevelt was 42, Franklin Roosevelt was 51, John Kennedy was 43, and "old man Ike Eisenhower" was 62.

These men did amazing things both before and while they were Presidents. Some people believe most people during the late 1700s died in their 30s-50s. Washington died at 67, Adams at 90, Monroe at 73, Madison at 85, and Eisenhower at 78. Kennedy and Lincoln were assassinated.

Teddy Roosevelt had an encyclopedia of injuries, bad habits, and illnesses throughout his life: asthma starting in childhood, malaria, accidents, infections, broken bones, arthritis, lumbago, diabetes, was shot in the chest in an assassination attempt, and it was rumored that he often ate 23 hard-boiled eggs for breakfast. It was surprising that he made it to 60.

Franklin D Roosevelt also had a long list of health issues throughout his life: polio, hyperesthesia, dysfunction of the bowel and bladder, facial and symmetric ascending paralysis, cardiac failure, acute bronchitis, and fevers. None of these illnesses or the fact that he spent years in a wheelchair kept him from his inspirational fireside chats that the nation depended on for mental and physical guidance during World War II. FDR's New Deal projects included the Tennessee Valley Authority, the Civilian Conservation Corps, the Works Progress Administration, the Securities Exchange Act, the Emergency Banking Act, the end of Prohibition, the

Social Security Act, and the Glass-Steagall Act. (Under the Clinton Administration, the Glass-Steagall Act was partially repealed, and that repeal would eventually cause the Great Recession of 2007-8.) Yes, FDR died at the young age of 63, but no President has worked more for the struggles of the common man. Society still reaps great benefits from these programs.

Eisenhower's life was filled with many common American experiences that endeared him to the populace: fishing from local lakes and rivers, gardening and selling vegetables from a cart he hauled through town as a child, animal tending for family consumption, camping, and vast military leadership positions and responsibilities. He spoke clearly to the public with a "liberal attitude towards the welfare of the people and a conservative approach to the use of their money as a basis of how one should govern." (Budget message to Congress 1/17/1955) He also wanted to strengthen Social Security and increase the personal health of the country's citizens to create a better society for everyone.

So here is a big question. Why are we still electing and reelecting great-grandfathers who have been running for political offices or those who have owned mega-million or billion-dollar businesses their entire lives to be our Presidents? Far-left beliefs for a leader are as bad for the country as the beliefs of the far-right. You cannot develop a country of states that are united through extremism unless you believe that people like Hitler and Stalin were good leaders for their countries.

When you put much older politicians or businessmen into office, they always come with an excess of long-term "baggage" associations that are mostly connected to the richest of the rich, with local or national business-people or they are indebted to longtime political cronies and/or corporate/political powers that have backed them for decades.

America's two political party's propaganda ads have also become abusive and hateful. The party not in power tells the American people that the party in power has policies that are failures, whether they have been failures or not. They tell the voters that real change can only occur when their party runs the government. Politicians blame everyone else but themselves for social or governmental problems, even if the problems occurred during their administration. Why not elect people who live and act more like America's common man or woman?

Look around our country. What is really going on? Have we become a nation where the ones with the most amount of money or power are always destined to become our political leaders? In practice, this is called a meritocracy, where the power of wealth and social position determines social and political outcomes. Are these activities supposed to occur in a democratic republic whose majority of citizens are struggling in our middle and lower classes? Meritocracy is now widely occurring in America. When you elect very rich people with large corporate or financial backgrounds, their general focus will be enacting legislation that, based on their biased perspectives, will benefit corporations the most. Adam Smith, the founder of American Capitalism, believed in the 1700s that this practice would be valid and mandatory in establishing wealth creation for the economic elites, who he felt should control the economy.

Think about this economic reality. What power and privileges are automatically created when corporations have budgets and financial capabilities that are greater than the budgets of many American cities or states?

Why not elect individuals who are teachers, nurses, carpenters, or small private individual business owners to Congress? Do you think that they are not educated enough or that they only have common people's values, which are not good enough to govern? It was common people's values that created our country in the 1700s. A lot of our average citizens are much more ethical and honest than many in Congress today.

There is one other aspect of politics today that our Founding Fathers feared, and that is the influence of extremist religious beliefs that could influence not only the creation of rules and regulations for governing the populace but also limit the ability of political compromise to exist. Most citizens today do not know or remember Barry Goldwater, a former major general in both the United States Air Force and Air Force Reserve from 1941 to 1967, who fought in World War II and Korea. He was a former United States Senator from Arizona for decades, and he was the Republican Candidate for President in 1964. He said something prophetic in 1981 that applies to what seems to be occurring in Republican politics today.

"Mark my word, if and when these (Evangelical) preachers get control of the (Republican) party, it's going to be a terrible damn problem. Frankly, these people frighten me. Politics and governing demand compromise. But these Christians believe they are acting in the name of God, so they can't and won't compromise."

ECONOMICS

A major proven theory of economics says that you should save money when times are good so that when times are bad, you will have more stability in your economic life. During the last 125 years of American history, this economic philosophy was more participatory after World War II because American citizens who lived before, during, and soon after the war knew what living with less or without meant.

Struggling has been a very important lesson for American citizens as the country ages. When people struggle, recovery is a more naturally fulfilling experience. Appreciation for what one has and thankfulness for positive parental influences have lasting meaning in one's life. Paying attention to the hardship experiences told to children by parents and grandparents, or even just reading about the struggles of American pioneers, widens one's understanding of how inner strength and dedication can be achieved on a personal level to overcome just about anything. Knowing how historical common sense works for many who have had to bear with and overcome adversities on their life journey can inspire great achievements in a person, a family, or a nation. What about now?

The more that people listen to and follow advertisers' propaganda that they need this car, this food, this drink, this type of clothing, this drug, or this type of home to satisfy their habitual social status and behaviors, the more money they will waste and the richer the corporate manufacturers become. Looking, acting, and thinking like all your friends do not express your uniqueness as a person. It manifests addictive behaviors.

The more a person believes that one or certain politicians have the remedy for solving all their problems, the more you will treat them like a god and the more you will do whatever they ask of you. When a person abandons historical common sense, the closer they become robotic pawns of the economic elites. Are we heading towards a culture that will eventually demand that computer chips be implanted under our skin so we can wait for the next signals from mega AI computers that will advise and instruct us on what is best for our personal identity and what to buy or do to satisfy our desires? Will using our God-given brains to comprehend and analyze our daily options become too tedious? Will we abandon our ability for introspective thinking because it consumes too much of our time and mental energy? Why struggle when our magic screens can provide us with the only answers we truly need?

The fear of losing individual identity in a fast-paced world was one of the major themes of George Orwell's futuristic-looking 1932 book "Brave New World."

CLASSICAL THINKING AFTER WORLD WAR II

In recent times, classical economic philosophies were more participatory for a few decades after World War II. Most citizens believed that if you were honest and responsible, over time, the leaders in Washington would expand, rebuild, and restructure American factories and businesses into building long-lasting, durable, high-quality merchandise and homes that an average person could afford and use for a long time to benefit their newly developing families. All the quality armament and warplane manufacturing skills America used during the war were transferred to building cars, homes, factories, and transportation facilities.

During this time frame, most families were helped by a generalized sensibility that all family members played a role in contributing what they were able to for the benefit of everyone in the family. Television programs were mostly about the joys, trials, and tribulations of average families and how solutions arose from the combined efforts of all family members. There were also programs about American pioneers, shows about soldiers' lives in and out of combat roles, and 1800s western adventures, as a few examples. There were many quiz shows, variety shows, and even a show called "Queen for a Day" that would honor hardworking women in struggling families for what they had accomplished through sacrifice and hard work that helped keep their families together.

The American Western TV show "Wagon Train" was so popular and morally educationally for viewers in the 1950s and 1960s that when Gene Roddenberry promoted his idea of a TV series called "Star Trek," he called it "Wagon Train to the Stars." (Wagon Train can still be seen on the FETV channel, the INSP channel, the GFAM channel, and Starz.)

Most programming on TV didn't feature decadence, mass murder, things exploding around every corner, or the over-sexualization of both men and women. They were mainly about how a person or a family could learn from their mistakes and develop harmony in their lives, often reflecting on people's family history or the lives of historical Americans.

If you want to watch a current TV show that takes a more moral, ethical, and historically classical approach, watch the Canadian TV series "Murdoch Mysteries" on Acorn, Ovation, or Acorn through Amazon. This show, set in the late 1800s to early 1900s, incorporates police work, new science, plus using the input of historical and scientific pioneers who exhibit a balance of morals and ethics in their efforts to help others.

PBS and The History Channel produce many types of programs that utilize a more Classical Education approach for entertainment and learning experiences. Contributing to PBS lets you watch decades of their shows.

Much of what you see on television today seems to take the opposite perspective compared to most of the shows of the 50s and 60s. So many of the programs seem to be about competitiveness: the best-looking or sexiest, the most daring and adventurous, the richest, and those most able to crush or manipulate the competition to achieve a win. There are also shows displaying which contestants can be more outlandish than other contenders. Abnormal extremes then become normal behaviors.

CULTS, COURTS, AND CONSTITUTIONS

When you believe that what one political party's propaganda tells you is the only truth and path you should follow, you have just joined a cult. Cults tell you that not only should you believe what their leaders tell you, but that you have every right to overwhelm or condemn the opposition because these others are the evil ones who are trying, for example, to destroy the Constitution of the United States. Yet, most American political cult members have never read the entire Constitution.

Being a Supreme Court Justice or a member of Congress in the United States does not forbid you from being a cult member. If you think rulings by the Supreme Court are the fair and last word in interpreting the American Constitution, think again. In 1776, the Declaration of Independence, written and approved by the Founding Fathers, proclaimed that in God's eyes, "all men are created equal, that they are endowed by their Creator with certain unalienable right that among these are life, liberty, and the pursuit of happiness." And the Founders said that these truths are self-evident. Wow. SELF EVIDENT. Then came the U.S. Constitution in 1789, which was written to primarily favor those citizens with wealth, followed by the Bill of Rights in 1791.

But in 1857, 68 years after the U.S. Constitution and 81 years after the Declaration of Independence, the United States Supreme Court ruled that Black people were never to be included as citizens and therefore, could not vote in elections nor have any of the rights and privileges of white citizens. I guess the Court felt that what the Founders thought was self-evident in God's eyes in the Declaration of Independence, which citizens fought for in the American Revolution, was now irrelevant.

Maybe you are thinking that this Court ruling was just an "out of the ordinary" event. Guess again. Since 1810, the United States Supreme Court has overturned its own precious "precedent rulings" between 145 and 230 times as of 2020. The number varies because of the intricacies involved in the wording of the rulings and other factors. I guess the Supreme Court isn't always correct in how they interpret the laws of the land. Maybe biases, prejudices, and religious beliefs might have clouded their judgments 145-230 or so times.

The overall Judicial system in the United States is extremely costly, very slow-moving, and inadequately financed and managed by most governmental bodies in this country. Many people have spent years and decades in jail for crimes they did not commit, especially if they were Black.

There are many citizens who were put in jail for something that was severely punished in one state, yet take five steps down the highway, and you are in another state where the same activity is not illegal at all.

What about when an identical crime is committed in one state by two men, one poor black and one rich white? The rich white guy gets one year or no time in jail for his crime because he can hire the best lawyers, draw the case out through numerous appeals, and pay whatever bail amounts or fines are set. Meanwhile, the poor black guy may not be able to make bail, hire a good lawyer, or file numerous appeals. This may result in him spending the next ten years in jail. This is how our current Judicial system in America defines "all men are created equal."

Our Judicial system was even more unfairly administered from the late 1700s to the late 1800s concerning legal treaties with Native Americans. Most of the treaties between America's original indigenous people and the American Government were either broken, violated, or not enforced. The fate of Native Americans almost became just a killing game where white-skinned people were not punished for killing Natives.

In 2022, the poverty rate of Native Americans was over 25%, much higher than it was for Black Americans. Life expectancy for Native men in 2021 was 62, and for women it was 69. Life expectancy for white Americans in 2021 was 73.2 for men and 79.1 for women. Why are we still abusing these people who lived on our lands before white people got here?

There is one more point I would like to mention about how one part of the Constitution's Bill of Rights was written and how one of the Amendments has been adjudicated by the Supreme Court. Our Founding Fathers based how they formulated many of the rules and rights in the Bill of Rights on what was then known as science, industrialization, and invention in the late 1700s. For example, back in those years, a skilled marksman could fire a rifle 2-3 times a minute, whereas now a gun can fire 2 rounds per second (120 rounds per minute.) A bump stock AR-15 can fire more than 400 rounds per minute, and a machine gun can fire 500-1000 rounds per minute.

Imagine how General George Washington or any military force commander in the late 1700s would feel about guns and gun laws back then if someone could show them a gun that could kill their entire army on the battlefield in 5-10 minutes. Would Washington say, "Everyone over 18 or 21 should be able to buy, own, and use these weapons however they wanted?" Or might he say: "These super guns in the hands of the average citizen have the potential to destroy our children and families, our personal liberties, and the survival of our country."

AMERICA LOVES VIOLENCE

It is estimated from numerous studies that the average child in America sees about 200,000 acts of violence and 16,000 murders on TV before they are 18 years old, with 8000 of those murders coming by the time children finish elementary school. Research has shown that this amount of violence produces a desensitizing effect and the potential for aggression, especially among children. The increase in the amount of bullying that goes on in schools shows that something is negatively affecting the minds and emotions of youth. Do you remember "Clockwork Orange"?

Have you ever watched today's illusionary Pro Wrestling matches in person or on TV? These once-called "sporting contests" became popular with the public dating back to around 1900. Television stations show these unrealistic wrestling performances many times each week. The greater the number of phony injuries and verbal negations exchanged between competitors, the more the die-hard fans love it. Women are also competitors and are as foul-mouthed and mudslinging boasters as the men. Today, Pro Wrestling is no longer considered a sport; it is now called entertainment because the winners are preselected before the performances are acted out in front of the audience. This is an excellent example of visual, legalized violence. Entire families in the arenas become screaming fans during each match. Many of today's families no longer seem to feel that visualizing the physical violence of breaking chairs on competitors' heads or wrapping steel chains around opponents' necks to simulate strangulations has any negative effects on their children's behaviors, attitudes, or the bullying of their children's friends.

WHAT'S NEXT ON AMERICA'S HORIZON

Americans have two directions from which to choose how their future unfolds. First, we can follow boasting leaders who will promise us everything if we support their political, materialistic, or philosophical biases. These leaders include politicians, corporate executives, and cult figureheads who all value money and power over everything else.

The second major direction for our country is to seek prosperity, fairness, and equality for all citizens, regardless of race, nationality, or economic status, based on a foundation of positive morals and ethics.

While the mega-rich continue making huge profits, the income inequality between them and everyone else keeps widening. Maybe both the poor and the middle classes should demand a New Declaration of Independence, just as the colonists in 1776 demanded theirs from the British. This New Declaration, incorporated into a New Constitution, would be modified and clarified to include an emphasis to affirm that:

"We hold these truths to be self-evident, that all men and women of all ethnic races of any skin color are created equal, that they are endowed by their Creator with certain unalienable Rights, that among these are Life, Liberty, and the pursuit of Happiness. That to secure these Rights, Governments are instituted among Men and Women, deriving their just powers from the consent of the governed, and that whenever any Governmental activity or laws become destructive of these ends, it is the Right of the People to alter or to abolish it, and create a New Constitution, laying its foundation on such principles and organizing its powers in such form, as to them shall seem most likely to affect the Safety and Happiness of everyone." Imagine a society where everyone is treated equally!

Many of the biased politicians who affirmed the Declaration of Independence refused to put into the Constitution of the United States those words and ideals from the Declaration of Independence. Between the Declaration of Independence and the writing of the Constitution of the United States, America's new wealthy and power-hungry politicians realized that guaranteeing all the "endowed by God rights" from the Declaration of Independence into the Constitution would give the governed masses the expectations that the poor would be treated in the same way as the rich. After the Revolutionary War, such a potential shift to equality would be an anathema to what Adam Smith's capitalism was all about.

The carryover of many rich merchants, some of whom were once former elite British subjects but who were now a part of the newly formed American economy, wanted to adopt Adam Smith's format for capitalism. His primary economic focus was mainly advocated to benefit the wealthiest classes by giving them the ability to create monopolies that would subjugate the lower classes and keep them poor and needy.

For many years, elitism has been seen as a requirement for political and economic advances because America's elites have brainwashed the public into believing that accumulating great wealth was an indication of one's ability to do what is best for all its citizens. Today, if you look around the country, what you currently see happening with our society's massive disparities in income inequality is what you have gotten from believing that our rich, elite ruling classes know what is best for you and your family. It is sad that so many citizens continue to follow and believe what our monetary and political elites say is best for them. Much of the corruption and injustices you see in America have come from those same elites.

With the way the 1791 U.S. Constitution was formatted and written, most politicians and landowners were reassured that blacks were just slaves and Indians were just savages who did not deserve any social or economic ranking. At the time, many governing politicians felt this elitist view was proper and acceptable for nation-building and economic growth. With no backlash from the Federal Government, increasing the number of slaves and the killing of more Indigenous natives was interpreted as both normal and morally proper. Even the Federal courts continued their approval of this ideology.

America's new political elites, industrialists, and large landholders saw average, common folk as the forever social class of workers who were intended to be dependent on the favors of the landowners and businessmen. This is one of the basic principles of Adam Smith's economic philosophy. For centuries, citizens have been told that American capitalism is the best form of prosperity for workers, but is that true?

After the Constitution, unless you were the wives of the rich, average women were mostly seen as child producers who cooked men's meals, washed men's clothes, kept the house clean, and did the garden. They were viewed as too weak-willed and too busy at home teaching and rearing their children to be involved in big business and politics.

What surprises me is that over 230 years later, many women in America are still being treated as if they were freed slaves of rich landlords. It is women who do most of the work as child caretakers, domestic workers, home health aides, sewing machine operators, cooks, maids, food preppers, and laundry and dry-cleaning workers for lower wages. These are all jobs that used to be done by the slaves of America's elite, even going back to the days prior to Thomas Jefferson's plantation workers. Without the low-paying jobs being done today by women, rich men's lives would be in chaos, yet many of these women are not being financially treated well by the people who hire them. Once again, this differentiation of classes goes back to what Adam Smith believed was how American Capitalism would work best for the prosperity of the rich.

Job income equality does not exist in America, where women ARE STILL making 20-40% less than men for doing the same job. If less affluent people were in Congress, this might not be the case because some middle-class wives would be telling their political husbands to stop treating women as inferior to men. What do you think might happen if the wives of middle-class representatives in a new U.S. Congress were to tell their husbands to "do something about changing the issue of income inequality among women, or you can forget having sex with me until things start changing?" This is obviously not a politically correct solution and may not work because many men do not see anything immoral or unchristian about their use of prostitutes. Yet these same men vehemently oppose this same type of activity for their wives. But I do not see an uproar when very rich men and women use the services of another person to satisfy their sexual desires. Does having great wealth and power justify this activity?

We don't need a violent revolution in the United States. We need some type of self-induced introspective wake-up call to realize the historically wrong choices we continue to repeat today as citizens and governments. How did some of the early colonists start nonviolent reforms?

Before the Revolutionary War, patriotic colonists, especially women, got together and stopped shopping at British-owned stores to protest the unfair laws, taxes, and behaviors the British Government was demanding of the colonists. By 1768, Boston, Philadelphia, and New York residents were boycotting imported goods from England. They felt that the huge prices, tariffs, and taxes imposed by England on the goods were just feeding the pockets of corrupt British officials and shop owners. The colonial leaders in Boston urged the colonists to "save their money to save their society" by being frugal. Since women were important managers of the household budget, they played a valuable role in how the colonial economy functioned. They were encouraged to find local substitutes to replace goods imported from Britain. Family security was a reason given for slowing down or stopping the consumption of British goods.

Certain shops in Boston that sold imported goods from England were boycotted. If you considered yourself to be a patriot, you were to purchase products made in the American colonies. By August 1769, those individuals in Boston who had been disregarding the boycotts of foreign goods had their names placed on the front page of the local newspaper. These actions cut the importation of British goods in half.

Fast forward to a more modern time in America. Several decades ago, American corporations decided to close thousands of factories here and ship the jobs primarily to Mexico, where things could be made cheaper for greater corporate profits. These companies were not looking out for the welfare of Americans. They were looking to financially benefit themselves and their stock market shareholders.

At a 1992 Presidential Debate, H. Ross Perot said America would hear a "giant sucking sound" as American manufacturers left America and set up their plants in Mexico. Clinton, most Republicans, economists, and corporate leaders said Perot was wrong even though most of those in favor of the NAFTA treaty had never read it. Perot's warning turned out to be visionary. Forward seven years when Clinton announced that the United States would renew the most-favored-nation status for China, and the once forgotten giant sucking sound became a tornado. History repeats, but who cares? Certainly not the corporations whose profits skyrocketed.

I don't think that Americans understand China. In China, the Chinese Communist Party is the only ruling party in the People's Republic of China. China is not a Capitalist country; it operates under a socialist framework. China is also a one-party dictatorship where the Communist Party has a monopoly on everything. Here is a list of some of the Chinese governmental activities that currently occur there.

Imprisoning protesters - yes. Detaining 2 million people from religious groups, including Uyghurs, Turkic Muslims, Christians, Kazakhs, and Kyrgyz - yes. Monitoring citizens through cameras and Internet surveillance - yes. Sending spies to American colleges, governments, and businesses - yes. I could go on with more, but if you don't get my point by this time, you will never get it.

If you want to see America's corporate leaders suddenly wake up, stop buying Made in China merchandise, even for just a trial period of one year. Just buy American or buy Korean or Japanese products instead. All Chinese products you buy ultimately help to support the authoritarian monopoly of the Communist Party. Every product that you buy that is made in America benefits the American public.

But wait, there is a problem with Americans willing to stop buying Chinese products. Behavioral-addicted American shoppers cannot stop buying cheap, lower-quality Chinese products and foods, nor stop buying expensive smartphones and electronics made in China. Excessive Chinese buying addictions help support and economically develop a communist country that is one of the biggest environmental polluters on the planet. Do Americans find joy in supporting a Chinese dictatorship?

Then there is fentanyl, a drug that both bizarrely satiates American illegal drug addictions and kills about 100,000 Americans every year. Fentanyl and its precursor chemicals are made in China. Selling these products abroad benefits China's economy while it creates havoc in our population with great sorrow and destruction in American families.

One of China's main goals is to surpass America's number one standing in the world in both economic and military strength. Since China has been around for thousands of years, its leadership may have a greater understanding of how many nations that were once the strongest in the world destroyed themselves over time with excessive negative behaviors.

What products you choose to purchase in America will determine both the survival and prosperity of American workers and the survival and maintenance of your health. As simple and feasible as this statement may be, habitual buyers find it hard to believe it. America's addicted buyers of Chinese goods want their desires fulfilled. Even though many Americans may hate the concept of Communism, they feel free to call many members of one political party in America Communist sympathizers. Yet, they care less if many of the products they buy and favor are made in a Communist country by low-paid, suppressed people who live in company chambers smaller than middle-income American bathrooms. Some products Americans buy may even be produced in internment camps or jails.

For a lot of people in America, the show and tell of materialism is everything, except when it concerns their physical health. And this last factor is causing a "self-induced age of destruction" in the health of the American populace.

The American Covid experience showed us how true this statement is. Over 1.2 million deaths, and as of 4/13/2024, there have been 6.6 million hospitalizations.   (covid.cdc.gov/covid-data-tracker/#datatracker-home) Besides the damage Covid has already done, there are plenty of current and yearly statistics available concerning the number of Americans whose long-term negative behaviors cause them to die from heart disease, diabetes, strokes, cancers, alcoholism, and legal and illegal drug abuse. These statistics are way out of proportion compared to other industrialized nations. Yet few politicians will admit that we are a sick country, and most of our consequential health problems are self-induced by negative behaviors.

My grandparents, who lived through World War I, the 1918 Pandemic, the Depression, World War II, the Korean War, inflation, food shortages, and hunger, lived to be in their 90s when they died of natural causes. They mostly ate natural foods cooked by themselves and did manual labor most of their lives (originally growing up in small towns or on a farm in Eastern

Europe before coming to America), and they both expressed gratitude for what little they had. My grandparents were not unique nor out of the ordinary in how they lived. Everyone around them lived in similar ways, whether it was on a farm in Europe, an American apartment building in a big city, or eventually their own small bungalow home on a 25-foot-wide city lot.

There is another aspect of how people view the direction and importance of their lives. It involves how much time and energy is spent on screen addictions. Solutions are simple, but limiting screen time seems to go against today's new normal behavior that a continual connection by using screens gives people a better sense of satisfaction by being able to fully control the dialog where truth and honesty become irrelevant.

For decades, we have had hundreds of new products and conveniences to supposedly make our ways of living easier, less time-consuming, and more comfortable. Most people spend more time watching computer screens, television screens, and smartphone screens than any other activity in their lives, and this includes how many hours a day they sleep. Though screen time addiction is real, Americans refuse to accept this fact as a mental, emotional, or physical problem. Withdrawals from this activity can be emotionally and psychologically shocking for many people. People are afraid that by shutting off their electronic connections, they will be separating themselves from their groupthink participation with others. They falsely believe that if they miss out on one tidbit of data concerning what is going on with their friends, their family, sporting events, Hollywood movies, actors, or song-singing stars, they will feel left out, and this will create more depression in their lives. Why not try the following?

Shut down your smartphone for a day and spend some time observing the public as you walk around watching the behavior of average Americans. Doing this for a couple of days might get you to see how many people are walking around like zombies glued to their phones. Gather with your family for an evening dinner or picnic in the park with your phones turned off. Instead of watching the latest blockbuster movie, watch some black and white Turner Classic Movies on TV made during the Depression Era 1930s and during World War II that maybe your grandparents or great-grandparents lived through. Watch and understand the many ways that people can be happy with less stuff. Take a drive out into rural America. Go camping with a tent in a more isolated site without a cell signal instead of driving down the highway in a motorhome and then spending the night in an RV campground with hundreds of people glued to their phones and Wi-Fi. There are so many simple experiences still available that benefit personal introspection, and many are free or at minimal cost.

IDEAS THAT MAY HELP PUT MORE FOCUS ON CITIZEN NEEDS

When someone declares they are running for a political office, at that moment, they should be required to provide a multi-aspect written plan of what legislation they want to enact and how they are going to try and achieve those objectives by working together with politicians from all parties. All politicians, especially wishy-washy or vague no-comment types, should be required to make themselves available to being questioned by normal citizens instead of only talking to biased news stations or reporters. Abraham Lincoln did this in the White House several times a week while he was President.

Here is another idea that might shake fear into some politicians' lives. Currently, many nationally elected Congressmen live in mini-mansions in the surrounding Washington, D.C. area, and they spend a lot of time either back home campaigning for reelection or spending an excessive amount of time running around in junkets around the world, spending tax-payers money to make themselves look like big shots in Washington.

Why not build a townhome or condo complex where all members of the House and Senate will reside when they are doing the people's business in Washington for which they were elected? There could be large rooms for discussions, including an amphitheater for each Congressional branch where camaraderie could be exchanged. As many politicians favor building walls at our borders, they could build 30 to 50-foot-high steel reinforced concrete walls around the complex for privacy and safety. Maybe a complex like this might produce more compromises.

People, especially legislators, might laugh at this idea, but we elect our representatives to legislate, not be treated like aristocratic kings and queens of royalty. Since average Americans spend at least 30-50 hours a week working at their jobs, maybe our politicians should also spend at least 30 hours every week doing their Congressional jobs in Washington.

Here is another idea for change. Why not allow for real debates to be conducted in both Houses of Congress? Modern politicians do not debate; they orate through speeches. This is not real debating. True debating involves each side asking questions of the other side to get specific answers concerning the issues each side presents. In other words, what are their justifications for their positions? There should be multiple cameras on the floors of both legislatures showing everything that is going on among the legislators. The public has a right to know what their representatives are saying and doing for the benefit of the people or if they are doing it for re-election or fund-raising purposes.

WHAT ARE WE DOING TO OUR MINDS?

People have so over-loaded their minds by actively participating in social media's "like me" connections, thinking about their poor health issues and family problems, wondering if their income is keeping up with their bills and expenses, regretting events from their past, and fantasizing about their future, that both their mental and physical health is suffering. Imagine how the focus of their thinking might change if they were healthy, lived a slightly slower-paced lifestyle, ridded their lives of the over-abundance of "stuff" they no longer need or use, and realized that the past is unchangeable, and their future is in the choices they make. People's destinies are created by both their lifelong choices and their failures to make choices when commitment is necessary for direction.

There is another reason why there is so much confusing data in your brain that is challenging your ability to comprehend and understand it all. It is the result of the Technological Data Overload that people experience from the endless hours and days that our American culture spends watching all forms of transmitting screens. Every form of technological input that you are feeding your brain significantly impacts your ability to either comprehend or ignore both the positive and negative effects this overload of data is having on you. The ability to "digest the overload" can become cumbersome, destabilizing, and directionless as you stumble through a self-created life of confusing insecurities.

If you want to learn more about how your brain works and what all your screen time is doing to it, I suggest reading "The Shallows: What the Internet is Doing to Our Brains" by Nicholas Carr. Another book would be "Homo Deus: A History of Tomorrow" by Yuval Noah Harari, about data collection and where this is leading our societies. If you do not want to take the time to read a book, watch "The Social Dilemma," a Netflix movie, for a partial discussion on the effects of online overload.

Most people don't realize that a lot of what is going on in today's world of data extremism and its side effects was predicted in Alvin Toffler's 1970 book "Future Shock." He said that in the future, technological data would be so rapidly generated by society that it would overload people so much that they would start going insane. If this statement is not ringing your bell, think about all the mental health issues that have developed in America, especially among our youth since smartphones became popular. Think about the explosion of mass murders that have occurred in America in recent years from unstable minds. Every minute of every day, technological data is exponentially increasing, and the population is sucking it up like it was free candy, but few people understand the effect it is having on themselves and the nation.

In Toffler's book "The Third Wave," published in 1980, he talked about how marriage and family would change, the development of extremist cults, a chaotic economy, and how people would find new ways of looking at work, success, and sex. Take a few minutes to look around your current setting. In 1970 and 1980, Toffler predicted much of what is occurring today. This is just another example where learning from what was said or written in the near-term historical past, was ignored. These books were global best sellers. Forgetting history is not inconsequential.

Concerning one's health, though good information is readily available to improve one's health and well-being, people often ignore these choices because they might conflict with the propaganda advocated by food manufacturers or the social tribes they have joined. This can and does happen in any nation when both commercial advertisements and Internet platform ads focus on short-term gratifications instead of recommending products and approaches for solving society's current health issues.

Many of the latest American surveys show that most citizens feel that our country is going in the wrong direction, and they blame whatever party is in the White House for the problem. The sad truth is we are at this point in America's history because of our exaggerated lifestyles, our overeating, and the massive debt accumulation that people, families, and our government have created by their choices.

Americans don't seem to realize that inflation increases when you demand a higher wage. Eating more, buying more, doing more, and demanding to own more of anything INCREASES INFLATION. Yes, it's a ridiculous merry-go-round ride, but it all originates with how our rich corporate and political elites have set up American Capitalism to work best for them, but this system may not work the best for you.

With America's mental and emotional stability not being in a comfortable place these days, people come up with irrational reasons to explain their problems. "My husband caused the stress that made me eat a whole box of cookies or drink that entire bottle of wine by myself." "Everything is rigged against me, and I am powerless to do anything about it." "I just need more money, a nicer car, a beautiful, loving wife, a rich man to marry, a bigger home, obedient children, and I'll be happier and more satisfied with my life."

Isn't it about time that adults stop acting like children and instead focus on all the benefits a person can receive from a framework of maturity based on how people can positively relate to each other regardless of their political party, race, color, or religious beliefs? A life based more on using historical Common Sense may not make you a millionaire but may make you happier with what you currently have and who you are.

ARE WE SPEEDING TOWARD ANOTHER GREAT CALAMITY?

In 1978, Sir John Bagot Glubb, a writer of 20 scholarly books, wrote a book called "The Fate of Empires" about how many nations have risen to greatness but, over time, collapsed. He based many of his conclusions on studying various civilizations over the last 3000 years. He observed how nations grew more cohesive over time as they focused on racial identity, religious adherence, and basic human nature by predominantly using rationality and reason in their lifestyles and governance activities. These activities and outlooks developed social harmony and nations that prospered. Glubb found that after the ages of "pioneers, conquests, commerce, affluence, and intellect" had occurred came the ages of "decadence, decline, and collapse." Some of the aspects of the collapse phase of a nation are now occurring in the United States: hard-working foreigners entering the country willing to do physical work that local citizens are unwilling to do, people living from inherited wealth instead of doing dedicated manual work, lost goal outlooks creating pessimism among the populace, too much emphasis in life on materialism and frivolity, the excessive love of accumulating money, a disdain for the country's leadership and culture, and abandoning religious morals and ethics.

Suppose you want a positive change to come from our government. In that case, you will first need to change yourself: tone down and rid yourself of negative attitudes or whatever addictive behaviors you may have that are stopping you from becoming healthier and happier. Governments reflect the behaviors and biases of both its leaders and the public.

It's been five years or so since the pink cloud was destroyed on orders from the then President. After the explosion, the citizens of the United States experienced a shower of tiny pink pellets that fell over America. The best scientists in the country could not find anything toxic about the pink pellets, and in a couple of days, the pellets just seemed to evaporate into the air. The general population rejoiced over the disappearance and framed the event as something insignificant in their lives.

Though some people thought the pellets were an "omen-esque" event, the vast majority quickly disregarded what happened. But as it turned out, the pink rainfall from the heavens did more to change the social, emotional, and economic life of American citizens than any other event in America's history. Over time, the never-experienced "pink fallout" created a mental outlook virus that induced genetic mutations and alterations in both the minds and physical bodies of those Americans who exhibited either extremist liberal political/social beliefs or extremist conservative political/social beliefs in their behaviors. The number of deaths that the pink virus caused these two groups was much larger than what had occurred with Covid. Unlike Covid, age did not seem to factor in the tens of millions who died.

The loss of large numbers of politicians in the United States Congress, the Judicial Branch, the Executive Branch, and individual state and local governments left large vacuums in leadership positions across the country. When the remaining politicians looked across the land, they soon recognized that compromise might be a lot easier now with all the extremists gone and with no similar believers taking their place.

The remaining middle-of-the-roaders decided that a New Constitutional Convention should take place to rewrite many of the laws and regulations that had previously been advocated for and passed by former extremist leaders throughout our history. Most of these laws had been created to mainly benefit themselves and their rich benefactors and corporate friends instead of helping most average Americans.

In the New Constitutional Convention, these centrist politicians decided that America should write into law many of the original ideals that Jefferson had written into the Declaration of Independence, which had emphasized the importance of having all citizens be fairly and equally valued and treated in all political, social, and economic activities.

The people involved in framing the New Constitution felt that all citizens should be held to the same standards of morals and ethics and regulations and laws with no exceptions. This included the President, all members of Congress in the House of Representatives and Senate, all Supreme Court justices, all branches of the Armed Forces, and any Federal workers associated with these groups. If you were going to represent or work for the different branches of our government while receiving a decent salary, healthcare benefit, and pensions, for example, your focused work behaviors should be positive examples that average citizens could emulate and respect.

As a result of many changes that took place, many public works projects, like those used in the Great Depression of the 1930s, were created to clean up the environment, improve the transportation system, and tear down and rebuild the crumbling, distressed, and crime-ridden inner cities. More acreage was set aside for larger parks and recreation areas for citizens to connect with nature.

Instead of mainly having an overemphasis on drilling for crude oil to make gasoline, a new focus was added for ethanol production made from growing sorghum, barley, sugar cane, and switchgrass-type vegetation. The power output of engines in many smaller vehicles was improved to increase fuel economy, and mass transit was expanded across various areas of the country. Hybrid vehicles were emphasized over pure electric vehicles until a better electrical grid system was built. All gas-powered vehicles were now tested for emissions and fluid leaks. A lot of young students and adults went back to riding bicycles to local stores and schools when safer bike paths were created. There was a big push to increase physical exercise among youth in all schools, and older citizens were encouraged and challenged to develop walking as a simple exercise routine for all ages.

Nutrition and healthy eating courses were taught in all K-12th grades. Junk foods were banned from being sold or served in schools that received federal assistance, and state governments were encouraged to incorporate healthier foods in their food service facilities. Single-use plastic containers and utensils were banned.

Monopolistic technology companies and social media platforms had to conform to the same rules and regulations that Print and TV companies had to follow concerning displayed content and language. Most public college tuition costs were greatly lowered because studies found that many expenditures were not helping to create better educated graduates.

Teachers were instructed to focus on a more comprehensive and common-sense approach to learning. Administrators finally realized that many young students worldwide were surpassing American children in academic achievements, so several areas of study received more emphasis and financial backing to compete better with other students worldwide. Too many colleges had been producing graduates in fields of study where the alumni had difficulty finding jobs in their specific fields. This necessitated changing course curriculums to fit social needs.

Specialized colleges were created to teach these other fields of learning with greater emphasis put on generating more grade school and high school teachers whose current ranks had rapidly dwindled by the retirement of instructors after their many decades of service. Universities and colleges finally realized that too many non-teaching junior and senior administrators and school reputation marketers were being paid to bolster a university's status and recognition. AI shortened the need for these jobs and other types of faculty positions where computers and machines could do the job faster and more efficiently.

In medicine, all over-the-counter and pharmaceutical drugs consumed by the public were re-evaluated for their efficacy, addictive possibilities, and necessity. Without extremists ranting and negatively stirring up the masses with falsehoods about drugs, politics, investment scams, or commercial products, society's stress levels rapidly decreased. With the New Constitution emphasizing the importance of citizens exhibiting more positive moral and ethical idealism, a calmness settled over the population. People finally understood how extremist propaganda from political parties was unnecessarily over-exciting their emotions.

Most politicians and judges finally realized that not only was the average citizen just as important as the biggest corporation, but in many instances, the welfare of the citizens was even more important. Factories were moved back to America from various countries, so the average citizen had more opportunities for a family's economic stability. Corporate leaders were now making 5-25 million dollars a year in salary and compensation instead of $100-200 million. Economic inequality started decreasing. Corporate buybacks were discouraged, eliminated, or taxed.

Those who were already wealthy remained wealthy, but there was a greater emphasis among them to financially help initiatives like Habitat for Humanity or other projects that built small or tiny homes for American veterans and families who were living on city streets in tents or cars.

Both federal and state governments set up 400-1000-acre farmland tracts all over the country that were set aside to professionally train and employ many less educated people to provide additional healthy fruits, vegetables, and lean meats to be sold at reasonable prices to the public. The words "locally grown" and "organically produced" encouraged both healthier soil stability and more flavorful food production. These numerous, smaller-scale experimental production facilities generated more pride and a greater sense of accomplishment among the workers. There was a cap set on the number of people in each small community because allowing too many people in a set space would degrade the benefits and lifestyles of those workers. Similar communities were popping up all over the country. (Exemplified in the 1934 movie: "Our Daily Bread")

So many positive changes were being introduced every day that people started looking forward to reading newspapers and watching the news on television about all the good things happening around them. Depression among students and adults started rapidly decreasing. Students now had the option in high schools to learn trade skills in carpentry, plumbing, auto mechanics, electrical installation, and other occupations for satisfying careers. All the students were given cell phones with only a calling function to communicate with each other and family members or for emergencies. With this one change, bullying virtually disappeared among students. Parents could buy smartphones for their children, but these were banned from use on school property. Abusive smartphone users faced punishments.

When people started reflecting on the arrival of the pink cloud near the Capitol years ago, they started calling the event by various names: the Second Coming, an Act of God, and even the Wisdom and Natural Power of Mother Nature. Whatever positive results occurred because of the pink cloud's appearance in the United States became a model to the rest of the world of what is possible in a society using historical common sense and middle-of-the-road thinking to better care for their citizens and how a country could more positively plan its future direction.

People started talking kindly to each other and making friends on mass transit vehicles instead of everyone around them having bent down heads, constantly looking at their cell phones. The New Constitution mandated balanced budgets for all Federal Government Agencies. Life in America became a place that was happier with more economic stability.

"Tom, Tom, do you hear me? Wake up!" said Tom's wife. "Come on, Tom, get out of dreamland and WAKE UP!"

"Huh, what? What time is it?"
"The country is going crazy, wake up and watch the TV."

All the news stations were reporting that some high-ranking person in the Internal Revenue Service had a meltdown and had been releasing and downloading to the Internet the last several years of tax records of all the people in the U.S. House of Representatives, the Senate, the Executive Branch and the Cabinet, the Supreme Court Justices, and the CEOs and most highly paid executives of the top 500 companies in the S&P 500 Index.

It didn't take long for average citizens to start forming protest groups against what they felt was economic decadence, abuse of power and influence, and unethical behaviors by both the wealthy and their political friends. Politicians were making millions because they were receiving inside information on stock opportunities, and corporate executives were making millions on upcoming government projects leaked from their political connections before the information was made public. It was also discovered that big banks and some corporations were secretly funding greater numbers of politicians and judges to persuade them to enact laws more in their favor. Thousands of citizens were surrounding politicians' homes, demanding fairness for average Americans and changes in

Congressional moral and ethical codes to stop the politicians from being bought off in numerous ways by rich corporation and lobbyists.

People were traveling to Washington, D.C., by the millions, demanding answers from their political leaders by blocking roads. Tens of thousands of protesters were willing to be arrested and taken to jail to show just how serious the current situation was.

Television networks had reporters interviewing citizens on the streets of every small town and major city in the country.

"Why do the super-rich have to live such decadent lives, never happy with millions? They need billions to feel good about themselves," said a 74-year-old disabled woman living on $1,000 a month Social Security, "I'm cutting my medications in half just so I can put food on the table."

"I'm an 81-year-old Army vet. Got drafted and served ten years in the service. I'd love for politicians to see what it feels like living in my wheelchair. Hardly any of these politicians ever served. Their daddies and money got them exempted. We were just made pawns for their war mania failures."

"My 8-year-old baby girl was killed by a drive-by shooter they never caught. Where's justice for me? It's just a joke. Violence and drugs all over the neighborhood. I never see cops on the streets protecting us poor folks. Talk is cheap; promises mean nothing, and crime gets worse. Politicians don't even come to my area anymore; they're afraid, just like me."

"Neither Republicans nor Democrats are enacting or enforcing laws to stop the mass shootings across America," said one small business owner whose store had been robbed several times by people with guns. "Decent citizens have just become fodder for the mass murderers to kill and maim whenever and wherever they want. Do you think maybe politicians might change their attitudes if they were the ones being slaughtered by gun-happy killers instead of us?"

Reporters at airports were watching many politicians and business leaders getting on private corporate jets that were flying them out of the country. They told the reporters the trips were for government research or corporate business, but they were afraid, especially when they saw screaming citizens in the thousands running toward their jets. It didn't take long for an average citizen to finally realize how the economic and political systems were rigged against them, where the top 10% of the population, who now owned over 90% of America's wealth, would never be content until they owned it all.

The Federal and State Governments didn't have the ability or space to arrest hundreds of thousands of angry protesters who refused to leave Washington, D.C. and state capitals. Since the demonstrators were not rioting, destroying, or occupying government buildings, the police forces did nothing to disperse the crowds. After several weeks, the demonstrators got hungry and fatigued from sleeping on the ground, so most of them left the areas saddened and disgusted. The congressmen had abandoned them.

Congressional people slowly flew back home, and corporate executives had their limos returning them to their offices. Like past protest experiences, politicians in government and corporate power positions started promising the public that they finally understood what people were complaining about during their latest protests.

Every leader in politics and business started repeatedly using the word "change" whenever they spoke to any newspaper, TV network, or YouTube Internet postings. These leaders, in numerous discussions with each other, knew that the protests would end quickly if they just let the camping out American protesters spend a couple of days in withdrawal from their normal addictive behaviors. They knew that in today's culture, prolonged, hard-core protesting in person was out of the ordinary and just a momentary pause in most people's lifestyles. After several days in the summer sun, people needed to get back to their wine, fast food services, 65-inch TVs, recliner chairs, unwholesome snacks, friend-me-friends, TikTok videos, and credit card purchases.

So, over time, those once justifiably angry American citizens had calmed down. Common Sense went back to being uncommon when politicians once again convinced their hard-core tribal believers that it was only their tribe who had all the right answers for everyone. The technology giants knew that with the new advances in the implantation of AI computer chips in people's arms, surrealism would potentially become everyone's new normal, filling each person's life with a never-ending kaleidoscope of fiction, falsehoods, and fantasies: more tech, more profits, more abilities to separate those at the top from everyone else.

It became easier for those in political and corporate power positions to control this newly structured, advanced technological, chip-in-arm class of "puppeteered pawns." Now, all Truths, morals, and ethics were fungible, only defined by how an individual feels about themselves at this moment as they progress in their daily search to quickly satisfy any of their immediate cravings.

At some point, someone wrote a SCI-FI book about an entity arriving on a pink cloud, hoping that people might wake up from the fantasy life they were living and maybe start doing something to advance America's historical, moral, ethical, and spiritual consciousness. Until that time comes, technology companies will become the go-to gods and guides for the future of mankind.

Implanted AI chips became humanity's quick solution and salvation from having to exert any type of manual labor or sincere personal effort to accomplish a task. AI soon replaced millions of people who had once sought historical economic freedom by doing focused and dedicated manual and office work while saving for their future needs. Why think about needs when all your wants are satisfied in seconds with AI chip computers and virtual reality headsets? With a culture that relies on immediate gratification to satisfy egos and desires, pseudo heaven-on-earth experiences were available 24 hours a day. Why go anywhere when you can have unlimited sexual fantasies or adventures to anywhere, at any time, with anyone while alone in your bedroom or office?

EPILOGUE

Why are United States citizens continuing to have poor health and unstable economic conditions in their lives? The answer is simple: the way the Constitution was written guarantees that Americans have the freedom to over-consume any foods, beverages, legal drugs, or smokable products which, over time, can cripple their bodies with diseases or other health problems. Our freedom also allows people to constantly make negative choices concerning their economic stability.

Americans also have the right to not exercise, sleep as little as they want, and buy whatever products they want even if they might not have the money to pay for them. We have the right to stay uninformed about how our bodies work or how the government functions. We can choose to not know our neighbors or care about what happens to anyone, anywhere in the world.

Unlike the Declaration of Independence, by the time the Constitution was written, the once favored Founding Fathers' moral or ethical behaviors of the Era of Enlightenment were not considered as important for governing the nation. Today, while morals and ethics are still preached from numerous pulpits and described in religious texts, many people do not consider using those qualities when choosing their options concerning their personal and financial health.

Some people in America have chosen healthier lifestyles. They have allocated more money toward savings and investments, controlled personal spending with balanced family budgets, took the time to get more sleep, didn't get involved in drug or alcohol overuse, lived within or below their means, got a good education (with or without attending college), and inspired their children with appropriate morals and ethics to guide them through life.

Maybe instead of listening to your heart and conscience, you chose to listen to the advice of a corrupt politician, a fantasy cult, or a pseudo religious leader. History has shown that many leaders who once preached that they knew what it would take to make their country great again, used tactics and behaviors that caused their country to eventually collapse.

We are living in chaotic times where both politicians and corporate leaders are using the internet, AI, and social media to lure citizens into accepting fungible truths and extreme "groupthink" ideologies as normal behavior. Are these activities the new road maps needed to achieve compromise and stability? History says no to this question.

With the way people's lifestyles are so overloaded with data and compliances, do they feel that personally analyzing and understanding their lives takes too much time and energy? Have people been so mesmerized by their phones, their virtual assistant boxes, and social media platforms that they believe technology will give them all the information they will need to navigate life's challenges?

When people lose or don't use their intuitive abilities to make historical common sense a valuable tool throughout their lives, they are giving up a natural God given talent that could make their lives happier and more stable. The solutions to many economic and health problems are readily available, but people need the belief and desire to open their minds to them and the fortitude to act on them.

BIBLIOGRAPHY AND RECOMMENDED READINGS

Albright, Madeleine "Fascism: A Warning" 218 HarperCollins

Barzun, Jacques "From Dawn to Decadence: 1500 to the Present – 500 Years of Western Culture Life" 2000 Harper Collins

Bonner, Bill "Empire of Debt" 2006 Wiles Pub

Boyle, T.C. "The Road to Wellville" 1993 Viking Press

Carr, Nicolas "The Shallows" 2010 W.W. Norton and Co

Degregorio, William "The Complete Book of U.S. Presidents"1993 Wing Books

Diamond, Jared "Collapse – How Societies Choose to Fail or Succeed" 2005 Viking Press

Eisenhower, Dwight D. "At Ease – Stories I Tell My Friends" 1963 Doubleday

Flake, Jeff "Conscience of a Conservative-The Rejection of Destructive Politics and a Return to Principle." 2017 Random House

Goldberg, Jonah "Suicide of the West" 2018 Crown Publishing Group

Giridharadas, Anand "Winners Take All- the Elite Charade of Changing the World." 2018 Alfred A Knoph

Harari, Yuval Noah "Homo Deus -a Brief History of the World" 2017 Harper Collins

Harvey, David "Seventeen Contradictions and the End of Capitalism" 2014 Oxford University Press, Penguin Random House

Heinlein, Robert "For Us the Living- a Comedy of Customs" Written 1938 Published 2003/4 Scribner

Hitchcock, William "The Age of Eisenhower" 2018 Simon and Schuster

Howe, Neil "The Fourth Turning is Here" 2023 Simon and Schuster

Landers, Ann "Truth is Strange" 1968 Prentiss Hall Ind.

Levitsky, Steven and Daniel Ziblatt "How Democracies Die": 2018 Crown Pub

Lewis, Michael "/The Big Short" 2010 Crown Publishing Group

Loewen, James "Lies My teacher Told Me" 1995 The New Press

Mallaby, Sebastian "More Money Than God" 2010 Penguin Group

Markel, Howard "The Kellogg's: The Battling Brothers of Battle Creek 2017 Pantheon Books

McCullough, David "The Pioneers" 2019 Simon and Schuster, N.Y.

Meyer, Dick "Why We Hate Us" 2008 Penguin Random House

Paine, Thomas "Common Sense" self-published 1776

Palahniuk, Chuck "Adjustment Day" 2018 W.W. Norton and Co

Public Papers of the Presidents 1953-1961 Washington D.C. 1960-1961

Reeves, Rochard V "Dream Hoarders: How the American Upper Class is Leaving Everyone In the Dust" 2017 Brookings Institute Press

Rosenthal, Dr. Elisabeth "An American Sickness" 2017 Penguin Pub Group

Sasse, Ben "The Vanishing American Adult" 2017 St Martin Press

Sax, Dr. Leonard "The Collapse of Parenting" 2015 Basic Books Pub

Straus, Willian and Neil Howe "The Fourth Turning" 1997 Penguin Random House

NOTES

[1] Merriam-Webster.com

[2] www.dictionary.com-wordorigins+history

[3] "Hitler: a biography" by Ian Kershaw 2008 New York W.W. Norton and Co. p.170,172,181

[4] Federalist # 10 by James Madison 11/23/1787

[5] The Northwest Ordinance of 1787 passed by the Congress of Confederation

[6] "The Pioneers" by David McCullough 2019 p.71-2 Simon & Schuster N.Y.

[7] Adjustment Day by Chuck Palahniuk p. 82, 295

[8] Theodore Roosevelt, letter to S. Stanwood Menken 1/10/1917

[9] Albert Einstein in "The World as I See It" 1934

[10] Rephrase of TV cartoon character Homer Simpson in "The Simpsons"

[11] "Why We Hate Us" by Dick Meyer 2008 p.19

[12] Ibid. (Meyer) p.20

[13] Ibid. (Meyer) p.32

[14] www.goodreads.com/authors/quotes/172293.Charles_J_Chaput

[15] "Suicide of the West" by Jonah Goldberg p.339-341

[16] Ibid. Suicide p.323

[17] "The Disappearance of Childhood" by Neil Postman quoted in "The Vanishing American Adult" Sasse

[18] Ibid. Sasse p.52

[19] Ibid. Sasse p.52

[20] Ibid. Sasse p 53

21www.dailymail.co.uk/Femail/article-2101786/my-soft-parenting-monsters-children.html

[22] "The Collapse of Parenting: How We Hurt Out Kids When We Treat Them Like Grown-Ups." Dr. Leonard Sax

23www.macleans.ca/society/the-collapse-of-parenting-why-its-time-for-parents-to-grow-up/www.quora.com

[24] www.asam.org/Quality-Science/resource-links/a-description-of-addiction

[25] www.strongnation.org/articles/737-unhealthy-and-unprepared

26www.cnn.com/2019/12/18/health/american-obesity-trends-welness/index.html

[27] www.bleacherreport.com/articles/2898840-nathans-hot-dog-eating-contest-
2020-joey-chestnut-sets-record-with-75-hot-dogs?utm_source=cnn.com&
Utm_medium=referral&utm_campaign=editorial

[28] "The Kelloggs: The Battling Brothers of Battle Creek" by Howard Markel 2017

[29] ww.historyworld.net/wrldhis/PlainTextHistories.asp?Historyid=ac65

[30] www.quora.com

[31] www.visualthesaurus.com

[32] www.christianity.com

[33] www.Christianitytoday.com

[34] www.biblestudytools.com

[35] www.vocabulary.com

[36] www.crosswalk.com article "What is the Sin of Sloth and Why Is It Worse   than Laziness." By Kyle Blevins

[37] www.the-ten-commandments.org/ten_commandments-purpose_meaning.html   plus a few additional words I added for clarity

[38] "Bishop Fulton Sheen: The First Televangelist," Time Magazine Monday April 14, 1952

[39] "Radio Religion" Time Magazine January 21, 1946

[40] David Harrell, "Healers and Televangelists After WWII in Vinson Synaan," The Century of the Holy Spirit: 100 years of Pentecostal and Charismatic Renewal (Nashville: Nelson 2001 p131)

[41] "A Colossal Fraud" Grace to You. www.gty.org/library/blog/B091207

[42] www.washingtonpost.com/news/wonk/wp/2016/01/31/this-is-actually-what-America-would-look-like-without-gerrymandering/?noredirect=on

[43] Henry Kissinger in The New York Times 1/19/1971

[44] Jerry Rubin in "Growing(up) at 37" 1976

[45] Milton Friedman in "Capitalism and Freedom" 1962

[46] "Unsafe Drugs Were Prescribed More Than One Hundred Million Times "in the United States Before Being Recalled" by Sonali Saluja, et.al The International Journal of Health Sciences, June 14, 2016

[47] "Seventeen Contradictions and the End of Capitalism" David Harvey, Oxford
    University Press 2014 p.171-2

[48] Ibid. Harvey p.173

[49] Ibid. Harvey p.171-3

[50] "World Happiness Report," from The Sustainable Development Solutions Network of the United Nations, 3-20-2020 Chapter 7 Introduction.

[51] "Sorry Bernie Bros but Nordic Countries Are Not Socialist" Jeffery Dorfman,
    Professor of Economics at University of Georgia, Forbes Mag. 7/12/2015

[52] Pope Frances Apostolic Exhortation November 26, 2013

[53] Pope Frances speech at Leon Sports Centre, Asuncion Condou, Paraguay July 12, 2015

[54] The Federal Reserve of the United States Chart of How Much Wealth is Owned by Who. "Distribution of Household Wealth in the U.S. since 1989" www.federalreserve.gov/releases/z1/dataviz/dfa/distribute/table/

[55] Congressional Record V.51 p.1447 December 22, 1913

[56] Federal Reserve Chairman Jerome Powell testifying before U.S. Senate Banking Committee June 16,2020

[57] "Ann Landers says: Truth is Strange" Ann Landers 1968 Prentiss Hall Inc

[58] "The Mindfulness Solution, Everyday Practices for Everyday Problems" Robert Siegal PsyD. Guilford Press 2009

[59] www.thoughtcatalog.com/jenna-lowthert/2014/10/10-simple-ways-to-achieve-true-happiness/

[60] From English Rock Group "Queen" song "I Want It All" from their album "The Miracle" 1989

[61] S.S. Alavi, et al. "Behavioral Addiction versus Substance Addiction: Correspondence of Psychiatric and Psychological Views" International Journal of Preventive Medicine. 2012 3(4) p.290-294

[62] United States Centers for Disease Control and Prevention. "Sexually Transmitted Disease Surveillance Report. October 2019

[63] United States Supreme Court. Zorach vs. Clauson. April 28, 1952.

[64] 1832. Cited in Jared Sparks, "The Life of Gouverneuer Morris" Boston, MA:
    Gray and Bowen, Vol. III p. 483

[65] President George Washington-Farewell Address Sept 17, 1796. "The Will of the People: Readings in American Democracy" (Chicago: Great Books foundation, 2001) p.38

[66] John Adams, "Letter to Zabdiel Adams, Philadelphia, 21 June 1776," in "The Works of John Adams – Second President of the United States," ed. Charles Francis Adams (Boston: Little, Brown & Co. 1854), 9:401

[67] Ibid. footnote 66. President George Washington

[68] Daniel Webster. Fourth of July Oration Delivered at Fryeburg, ME. In the
    Year 1802 (A. Williams & Co/A.F. & C.W. Lewis, Boston MA 1882) p.12

[69] Noah Webster. "Advice to the Young," History of the United States, (New Haven: Durrie 7 Peck, 1832), 338-340

[70] www.fas.org/Sgp/ors/misc/R45583.pdf. "Occupational Categories by Members in 116th Congress" July 22, 2020 Congressional Research Service

[71] www.en.wikipedia.org/wiki/The_Grace_Commission

[72] President John F. Kennedy Presidential Inaugural Speech. 1-20-1961

[73] "The Complete Book of Presidents" William A Degregorio. Fourth Edition 1993. Wings Books New Jersey

[74] Ibid. Degregorio p. 583-5

[75] Ibid. Degregorio. p. 605

[76] James Davidson Hunter, "Culture Wars: The Struggle to control the family, art, education, law and politics in America" 1992

[77] "The Starr Report: Narrative." Nature of President Clinton's Relationship with Monica Lewinsky. Washington, D.C. U.S. Government Printing Office

[78] www.fas.org/sgp/crs/natsec/IF11182.pdf Congressional Research Service

[79] www.wn.wikipedia.org/wiki/casualties_of_the_Iraq_War

[80] Roper Center 2009. Job performance rating for President Bush

[81] www.polingreport.com President Bush -Overall Job Faring in National Policy

[82] Presidential Approval Ratings – Barack Obama. Gallop Polls.

[83] "The Age of Eisenhower" William I Hitchcock. Simon & Schuster, p 6

[84] "At Ease: Stories I Tell Friends" Dwight D, Eisenhower. Garden City, N.Y. Doubleday 1963 p 31,68

[85] "Mandate for Change. 1953-1956" Dwight D. Eisenhower. New York. p.32

[86] Ibid. "The Age of Eisenhower" p. 16 Doubleday

[87] Ibid. "The Age of Eisenhower" p. 26

[88] Ibid. "The Age of Eisenhower" p. 27-8

[89] The Cleveland Plain Dealer. April 6, 1950 Philip W. Porter

[90] "The Chance for Peace" delivered to the American Society of Newspaper Editors, April 16, 1953

[91] Ibid. "The Chance for Peace."

[92] "Public Papers of the Presidents: Dwight D. Eisenhower" p. 89

[93] Ibid. "The Age of Eisenhower." P.256

[94] "Public Papers of the Presidents: Dwight D. Eisenhower" p. 313-318

[95] www.bloomberg.com/graphics/2020-highest-paid-ceos/

[96] www.usatoday.com/story/money/2020/05/19/50-highest-paid-ceos-in-2019/

[97] www.Equilar.com/reportstable-equilar-200-new-york-times-highest-paid-ceos-2019.html

[98] www.itep.org/notadime/#table

[99] "Public Papers of the Presidents: Dwight D. Eisenhower." p 140-141

[100] "Public Papers of the Presidents: Dwight D. Eisenhower." Farewell Address to the Nation. January 17,1961. p. 1035-40

[101] Eisenhower quoted in the Saturday Evening Post, April 21, 1962. p. 19